JACQUES LIPCHITZ · THE ARTIST AT WORK

Jacques

L I P C

The

Artist

at Work

H I T Z

by Bert Van Bork

with a critical evaluation
by
Dr. Alfred Werner

Crown Publishers, Inc.

NEW YORK

ACKNOWLEDGMENTS

Essentially, this book became a reality through the collaboration and approval of Jacques Lipchitz, who gave so generously of himself and of his valuable time. His gracious wife, Yulla, was always ready to answer countless questions.

In addition, I wish to acknowledge with gratitude the cooperation of the Museum of Modern Art and the Guggenheim Museum in New York City, as well as the Philadelphia Museum of Art, with my special appreciation to Sturgis Ingersoll, Chairman of the Board, and Henri Marceau, former Director, of the Philadelphia Museum of Art. Furthermore, I wish to thank Karl Katz, Director and Chief Curator of the Bezalel Museum at Jerusalem, Israel, for his enthusiasm and encouragement. I also wish to express my gratitude for the deep interest and perceptive advice of the late Otto Gerson. Special acknowledgment is due to Charles Benton for his earnest interest in the idea of this book and for his tireless efforts and valuable help in its behalf.

My special thanks go to John Spring, his sons, and his men at the Modern Art Foundry, Long Island, New York; and to Don Walkoe for his imaginative design of this book.

I have also received valuable information and assistance from Isadore Grossman, Larry Levy, and Robert Armstrong.

Last, but not least, I am grateful for the aid, devotion, and inspiration of my wife, Maria.

BERT VAN BORK

FOREWORD

*So many books have been published with black and white and good
color reproductions of works of art, and so many words have been written
about artists and their art, to come across an entirely original idea
in the field of art books is a refreshing and stimulating experience.*

*The concept of making a photographic record of the creative
life of the artist, his environment, his everyday activities, and even
his source of creativity is a valuable and essential form of
documentation. How fabulous it would have been if we could have
had photographs of ancient Greek and Egyptian sculptors at work, or
of Michelangelo creating his Moses and the Sistine Chapel paintings.*

*I have often had the pleasure of being in the company of
Jacques Lipchitz. He is an admirable human being and an artist to
respect. As with other extraordinarily creative individuals, much can
be learned and felt on various levels of contact with him.
His energy in a firm handshake or embrace is a release of human vitality
which is also inherent in his every work. The equilibrium
in his stance is echoed by the logical balance of his sculptures.*

*Lipchitz has a reverence for three-dimensional art. He explores
the plasticity of every man-made object to find its fundamental nature.
Most art dealers know Jacques Lipchitz as an avid collector of
ethnological objects and antiquities. Surrounding himself with
enigmatic and tantalizing pieces, he studies and handles the works to
learn more and more about his spiritual ancestors.*

*This quiet man who has absorbed the artistic heritage of many
centuries also has the religious history of millennia within him.
Lipchitz feels that behind everything there is a supreme being and a
power from which he derives his own strength.*

*After he had spent two emotion-crammed, exciting, kaleidoscopic weeks
in Israel, I asked Jacques Lipchitz if and how this visit, his
first to Israel, would affect his future work. The sculptor thought
and answered: "It will—but how, I don't know. I must wait and see
what I will make." This is honesty, integrity, and strength.*

*These qualities are visible in his art. They are relayed to us
through this unique assemblage of photographs—pictures of a man hard
at work, intensely occupied by his craft, creating with no
superficialities but straightforward and unmannered.*

*For the Bezalel National Museum, Jerusalem, this collection of
photographs will have great significance. This museum will one day be
entrusted with the lifework of Jacques Lipchitz. This concentration
of the artist's output will make it imperative for everyone
interested in his work to come to Jerusalem to study his versatile
efforts. The photographs in this book will aid the scholar and
general public by permitting them to peer into the artist's world.
They are a remarkable record—footnotes and insights, observations,
perceptions, and views—of a wondrous career.*

KARL KATZ   Director and Chief Curator
                                   Bezalel National Museum, Jerusalem, Israel

A BIOGRAPHICAL SKETCH

As the ship, in convoy, moved into New York harbor, the purple-gray mist of early morning lay across the deck. Gulls circled over the bow. Slowly, on the horizon, the skyline of the city emerged.

Along the ship's rails the passengers gathered. Some were Americans returning home, but most were refugees, coming for the first time. Among the refugees were Jacques Lipchitz and his wife Berthe. They had fled from Paris only a few months before. Excited voices mingled with the harbor sounds, the horns, the bells, the throb of tugboat engines. They were looking at the Statue of Liberty.

What a perfect greeting, Jacques Lipchitz thought to himself, France is reaching out to welcome us to the new land.

He walked with the crowd down the gangplank, wearing his only suit of clothes, indistinguishable from the hundreds of other refugees. In one hand he carried a portfolio of sketches, in the other a bag containing the sculpture *Flight*.

This was the way Jacques Lipchitz arrived in New York.

In other times it would have been very different. But this was June, 1941; the newspaper headlines and the thoughts of the country were anxiously preoccupied with the war in Europe. It was a chaotic time, and Lipchitz' arrival went unnoticed.

The outward circumstances of his journey were in many ways no different from those of other refugees. He, too, had stayed until the last moment, hoping that he would not have to leave his beloved Paris. When he finally did, he was only a breath ahead of the Germans, never knowing whether or not he would get away alive. Those were grim and despairing times, hiding out by day, traveling only by night, with always the fear of capture and the grim concentration camps to drive him on.

The Museum of Modern Art had sent their envoys to France to establish contact with a number of artists who were in danger of being captured by the Germans. When they finally found Lipchitz in the southern part of France, which had been declared a free zone, he did not want to leave. He knew nothing about America, and the prospect of living in a country where—as he believed—there were no trees, made him shudder.

It took a great deal of persuasion by his closest friends and by the American Consul to convince him of the grave necessity for his flight. Having left all his possessions behind— his house and studio, his work, and his valuable art collection—he arrived in America with only a handful of belongings and almost no money. But his heart was full of hope and the courage to start all over again.

In a small basement apartment in lower Manhattan he plunged into his work. Little actually changed in his new environment. The themes for his work had been conceived earlier. He wanted only to sculpture again, and America provided the freedom he so desperately needed. In the hustle of New York the war seemed far away. What was to become of those he loved who were still in Europe, caught up in the terrors of war?

He could not reconcile himself to the incongruity—his safety and their peril—or to his inability to help them. These concerns tormented him day and night.

The first sculpture he made in America was called *Arrival,* a companion to *Flight.* Then came *The Rape of Europe*—a new form, a different meaning from the sculpture with the same name that he had made in 1938. This time Europe was killing the bull, her ravisher. This symbolized his hope.

One of Lipchitz's first concerns, as he slowly adjusted to life in America, was to find a dealer to handle his sculpture. He sought out Joseph Brummer, who had given a showing of his work in New York several years earlier. But Brummer no longer handled modern art; he now sold antiques. Lipchitz was very discouraged by this — he had put all his hopes in Brummer. His financial situation was precarious, and without a dealer it would soon be desperate.

However, Brummer arranged a meeting with Kurt Valentin. Valentin had worked in a gallery in Berlin where he had handled some of Lipchitz' sculpture. He had left Europe several years earlier than Lipchitz and settled in New York, where he had his own gallery. Through the years Valentin had become the advocate and patron of many struggling modern artists. His foresight in modern art made him highly respected in American art circles. Valentin agreed to become Lipchitz's dealer, and in the succeeding years the two men became close friends.

Lipchitz was anxious to have a showing immediately. But Valentin's gallery was closed, most of his clients having left the city for the summer. Nevertheless, Valentin was able to raise six hundred dollars by selling several of Lipchitz's drawings, and they planned an exhibition for the fall.

Meanwhile, Lipchitz was offered teaching positions—professor of sculpture, lecturer in fine arts. But he felt that he could not do both — work and teach — so he declined the offers. Even when his funds were seriously low, only one thing mattered to him — he had to devote himself solely to making sculpture.

He moved into a one-room studio on Washington Square South. From his window he could overlook the green trees in the park, which he loved. Now he worked prodigiously, revitalized by the freedom and personal safety he was experiencing again. *The Promise, The Betrothal, The Bride, Spring Blossoming,* and the massive *Benediction* (benediction for the deliverance of France) emerged from his hands. Soon his studio overflowed, and he had to rent additional space.

In January, 1942, Kurt Valentin held an exhibition of Lipchitz's work. At a gallery nearby, the Dutch painter Mondrian, whom Lipchitz had met many years ago in Paris, was having an exhibition. Lipchitz went to see it and there met Mondrian again. They talked about their work. Lipchitz, however, is not an admirer of non-objective art.

"Mondrian was a marvelous man and a real artist. But I think that he understood painting in a different way than I did. I was astonished when he said to me: 'But, Lipchitz, look, don't you see that we are doing the same thing?' I had my exhibition at the same time, you know, and I had made things directly in wax, very free, very exuberant and full of life and passion. And his was such a cold, abstract thing. But, thinking about that later, I understood that he was absolutely blind to painting. It was something else that gratified him, because his painting was such a cold, calculated thing. It was even not painting, it had nothing to do with it, because the colors were not in their place; the reds were sticking out, the blacks were holes, and so on. It was not the language of painting that he was speaking. His language was absolutely foreign to me."

One day a young woman came to Lipchitz's studio to ask him to endorse some plasticine material. He told her that he was not concerned with material.

"Oh, how can a sculptor not be inspired by material?" she exclaimed.

As is often his way, Lipchitz replied with a story which he made up:

"Suppose Rembrandt were walking in the streets of Amsterdam, absorbed in his thoughts. Suddenly a friend passes him and calls out: 'Hello, Rembrandt, how are you?' It's an old friend whom he hasn't seen for a long time, a very good friend. The friend asks: 'What are you doing?' Rembrandt searches in his pockets for a crayon and paper to explain to his friend what he is doing, but he has none. They are standing in front of a huge white wall, and suddenly Rembrandt puts his finger into the gutter mud and makes a drawing on the wall. Imagine Rembrandt putting his finger into the mud and making a drawing which becomes pure gold. Now you can imagine anybody else making a drawing, putting his fingers in pure gold which becomes mud. So you see, the material is the man, the human being who is behind it!"

For Lipchitz this was profoundly important. In a period of war, when monstrous machines were destroying man, in an artistic period so dominated by calculated abstractions, the human element became, for Lipchitz, paramount. "Man must dominate over physical matter, the artist over his medium," he has said.

It was this search for physical freedom that had led Lipchitz years before to make his transparencies, to free his sculpture from the bonds of its own material. It was this same search for freedom throughout Lipchitz's career that led to the creation of a Prometheus who had broken the chains that bound him and was strangling the vulture.

In 1943 Lipchitz received a commission to do a sculpture for the Ministry of Health and Education building nearing completion in Rio de Janeiro. The architect, Oskar Niemeyer, had designed a large wall against which the sculpture was to be placed. This was the opportunity Lipchitz had been hoping for — to recreate his Prometheus, which he had made in the late 1930's for the Paris World's Fair and which had been destroyed later by the extreme reactionary elements in France. Since the theme of Prometheus was most appropriate for the Ministry building, he submitted a new sketch which was accepted. However, unfortunate circumstances and misunderstandings have caused Lipchitz to declare that the sculpture is not his.

The work had occupied Lipchitz for a year and a half. Its finishing touches coincided with D-Day, the Allied invasion of Normandy.

Soon Europe would be free. He poured his hopes into sculpture—*Happiness, The Joy of Orpheus, Song of Songs, The Rescue.*

When the war ended, Lipchitz looked forward to returning to Paris, and in June, 1946, he and his wife sailed for France.

Lipchitz's initial reaction was that Paris was the same — unchanged. But there was much sadness — many friends he had hoped to see were gone; many were dead. His dear friend Soutine, who had refused to come to America, had died in 1943 after being arrested as a foreign agent. Max Jacob, his companion through many a hardship, had been a victim of Nazi concentration camps.

During his stay in Paris, an exhibition called "The Masters of the School of Paris" opened at the Luxembourg Museum. Lipchitz attended the opening. Several of his works were being exhibited. As he stood at the back of the room, listening to the guide who was explaining his sculpture to the crowd, someone suddenly touched his shoulder.

"I turned around and there was Picasso! We embraced each other joyfully and said things to each other. It was like a dream — our eyes were filled with tears. Then we opened our eyes again, and we saw all those people standing around us and staring. We were suddenly somehow ashamed, as if we had made love in public, and we sneaked away."

His friendship with Picasso had been a long and affectionate one, dating from his early days in Paris. And the unexpected meeting brought back the vivid memory of those important years in his life.

During the first decade of the century, hundreds of young artists and poets came to Paris from all over the world, for Paris was then the nucleus of cultural and intellectual movements in the western hemisphere.

In 1909 Jacques Lipchitz arrived from Lithuania at the age of eighteen. He was shy, naive, callow. He knew and admired the classical sculpture of ancient Greece, but was unfamiliar with the young revolutionaries who were determined to replace the naturalistic image of man and his world with freer forms. The timing was perfect for Lipchitz — he arrived on the threshold of a new concept in art.

"I was completely raw material when I arrived in Paris. I didn't know anything. I had an itch which I had to satisfy. I wanted to work with sculpture, because I had been doing that in my childhood. I started to make things — why, I couldn't tell you — just an itch, that's all."

His mother had decided, without the permission or knowledge of his father, to send their eldest son to Paris to give him a chance to prove himself. Supported by the counsel of a local sculptor-friend, she sent him off with lots of good advice and a small amount of money — her savings — which would help him through the first few months. She promised to send more money later.

He enrolled at the Ecole des Beaux Arts and began to study sculpture under Jean Antione Ingalbert.

"It was futile in the beginning. But little by little I found myself, and then I really worked hard, very hard. Sculpturing, drawing, going to lectures and museums, all that. I was very homesick at first, therefore it did not go so well."

When his father consented to let him continue his artistic studies in Paris, a small allowance began to come in regularly. He then gave up his full-time enrollment at the Ecole des Beaux Arts and attended sculpture classes at the Academie Julian under Raoul Verlet, where he soon won first prize in a student exhibition. He returned to the Ecole des Beaux Arts only a few afternoons a week for classes in stonecutting. In the evenings he went to drawing classes at the Academie Collarossi of Montparnasse.

Eagerly, passionately trying to learn as much as he could about art, he spent his free time going to lectures and wandering through museums and galleries. Often he did not have enough money to buy a hot meal. But he felt a certain pride in sacrificing all material necessities for his obsession with art.

In 1912 he exhibited at the Salon National des Beaux Arts. The great sculptor Auguste Rodin visited the exhibit and expressed admiration for Lipchitz's work. But Lipchitz's artistic comprehension was still bound to classical sculpture, and he rebelled against Rodin's work. If my work receives Rodin's commendation, then something must be wrong with it, he thought. Rodin, who at that time was the undisputed master, almost represented a threat to the younger generation of sculptors. For this reason, Lipchitz rejected an offer to work as protege under Rodin. Rodin was not yet the genius he would become later to Lipchitz, after the young sculptor had grown more mature and perceptive.

Later that year he took a studio apartment at 54 rue du Montparnasse. The first night there he could not sleep at all. Through the wall of his studio came a monotonous, maddening tapping, like the dripping of a faucet or the scratching of a rat. Throughout the next day the noise continued.

"I asked the concierge: 'Who makes that noise?' She showed me a bearded man and said: 'That is Brancusi!' But I didn't know him; I didn't even know that he was a sculptor. So I asked her what he did, and she said: 'Go to the cemetery of Montparnasse, and there you will see a monument made by him.' I went and looked at it, but I did not like it. But after I saw his sculpture I knew how he made that noise, hammering and chipping away without rest."

In 1913 Lipchitz exhibited at the Salon d'Automne with a work called *Woman with Gazelles*, which received glowing praise from the art critics. Although happy over the statue's reception he was severely critical of his own work. He was turning away from classical Greek sculpture.

He was not satisfied to study the collections in the museums. He wished to have a collection of his own and through it to link himself with the art of all men and of all times. On Saturday mornings he wandered through the Marché aux Puces, the Flea Market of Paris. It became a ritual and a source of great pleasure to him. From his earliest days in Paris he became a passionate collector of art.

"You see, I am the son of a builder, an architect, and in our family my grandfather was always buying things that he liked, even when he did not know too much about them. And my father did, too. Probably I inherited this desire. When I came to Paris I wanted to have things around me, not alone to possess them but to learn from them. I knew that I had the patience for sculpture, but what it is and how to work at it I did not know. So I started to buy and have things around me. I still continue to do that. I am an incurable collector, you know."

Amid dusty piles of neglected, insignificant paintings at the Flea Market he sometimes found unrecognized treasures — a Rousseau, a Utrillo, a Goya, and later even a Michelangelo. These discoveries gave Lipchitz a tremendous satisfaction, for they meant that his critical knowledge of art, so slight at first, was growing. He was beginning to see!

During these years he met many of his future colleagues, among them Léger, Metzinger, Derain, Rivera. It was through Rivera that he met Picasso.

The Mexican, Rivera, at the time an ardent Cubist along with many other young avant-garde painters in Paris, revered Picasso. Picasso was the leader of the Cubists, but they interpreted their master's style in their own ways. Lipchitz, however, observed Picasso more objectively. One day Rivera took him to Picasso's studio. Picasso was not in, but the door was unlocked and they entered. Rivera showed Lipchitz around, pointing to each piece with great enthusiasm and pride, as if it were Rivera's own. His admiration for Picasso and his work was boundless. He pointed to a small bronze which was brilliantly painted (*Absinthe Glass*) and said to Lipchitz: "Voilà de sculpture!" Lipchitz did not like the implication in his voice. It sounded as if Rivera was saying: "Look here, young man, this is sculpture — what you are doing is not." But he decided not to argue with Rivera but to ask Picasso about it.

When Picasso arrived, Rivera introduced Lipchitz to him and Picasso responded very cordially. He spent some time showing them through his studio and explaining his work. Then Lipchitz asked:

"Mr. Picasso, how do you consider this little bronze? Is it painting or is it sculpture?"

"Well," Picasso replied a little sarcastically, "don't you know the difference between sculpture and painting?"

Lipchitz was embarrassed by the question and a bit insulted.

"Mr. Picasso, I certainly could not tell you what is painting, but one thing I can tell you — that's not sculpture."

"But why?" asked Picasso, startled. "Because it is painted? Look at this African mask on the wall, black with white rings under the eyes. Look—that's painted too."

"Yes, that is painted, but look how it is painted!" Lipchitz replied. "The white to me represents shadows. The mask is black, and the carver wanted to show shadows under the eyes. Of course, he could not make them black. On a white mask he would have made black shadows."

Picasso remained silent.

Rivera was furious. Lipchitz had insulted the master. When they left the studio, he turned on Lipchitz: "You peasant, you made Picasso angry!"

"Well, I couldn't stand his sarcastic answer. I told him only what I think. If he is my enemy now, there is nothing I can do."

Two days later, however, Picasso visited Lipchitz in his studio, and as time went on the two men became close friends.

Lipchitz was now turning away from the traditional forms based on classical sculpture. He was beginning to experiment, to test new paths. He completed *Woman with Serpent, Dancer,* and *Encounter*—all intense, kinetic works concerned with the problems of space and rhythm. But as yet he refused to let himself be influenced by Cubism. He wished to find his own path, his unique path.

In the early summer of 1914 Rivera organized a group of artists, Lipchitz among them, to travel to Mallorca for a vacation. They stayed in San Vicente, then only a few houses, now a well-known summer resort. It was a natural paradise for Lipchitz. He was overwhelmed by the haunting, beautiful Mallorcan countryside. Sketch pad in hand, he spent the days wandering along the donkey-cart paths of the island. At the foot of the hills, huge rocks leaped up from the placid blue sea. The vision of these rock formations was planted like a seed in his mind—a new geometry of forms that would soon be born in his sculpture.

The harmony of their primitive isolation ended abruptly with the outbreak of World War I. Many in the group had to leave immediately to fight. Lipchitz, having been rejected from the army because of ill health, remained in Mallorca for a few more weeks. Later he met Rivera in Barcelona and went on with him to Madrid. At the Russian Embassy he tried to borrow some money to allow him to return to Paris. The officials, however, informed him that this might take several months, so Lipchitz and his friends decided to move into an apartment on the Calle de Goya, near the Plaza de Torres. Rich with impressions of Spain, he began to work. The first piece he made was *Girl with Braid* for which he had done sketches in Mallorca.

Before they arrived in Madrid, Lipchitz and Rivera stopped in Toledo, where Lipchitz became fascinated with El Greco, who today remains one of his favorite painters. In Madrid he regularly went to the Prado and spent hours before the masterpieces of El Greco, Goya, and Tintoretto.

A Spanish friend introduced Lipchitz to the matador Joselito, a celebrated personality of his time. Lipchitz would often sit in Joselito's box at the Plaza des Torres. Often they rode together through the streets of Madrid in Joselito's elegant carriage.

"I lost my identity," Lipchitz remembered. "I became known as the friend of Joselito."

This friendship inspired him to make a statue of a bullfighter, and while still in Madrid he made sketches and began the sculpture.

When he returned to Paris in early 1915 he brought back with him the plasters of *Matador, Sailor with Guitar*, and *Girl with Braid*. However, severe financial difficulties were hindering his work. He had no money to have his plasters cast in bronze. So one day he went to see one of the best foundrymen in Paris, Monsieur Valsuani, and persuaded him to let him do his own castings in the foundry. Ever since, Lipchitz has continued to work in the foundry—supervising, adding, changing, repairing, and the like.

In the gloom of wartime Paris, Lipchitz plunged into his work with great energy and zeal. Now the Mallorcan impressions began to emerge from his subconscious and enter his imagination. Lipchitz began to work within the Cubist idiom.

One of his first sculptures in the Cubist idiom, however, proved to be a short diversion from the basic concepts that had formed in his mind. The sculpture *Dancer* was composed of flat wooden boards cut out and fitted together like demountable objects (a forerunner of constructivism). Of this experience Lipchitz remarks:

"In the beginning, around 1915, we Cubists went away from the anatomical aspect of the human body for our sculpture, and we had to find a new plastic anatomy which had really nothing to do with anatomy, which had to do with construction. And I was making such demountable sculptures, not like a sculptor and more like a cabinetmaker. I was going from organic to some kind of nonorganic life. I was abandoning nature altogether, and suddenly I became frightened. I was taking away and taking away—until there was nothing left but a stick. I saw the danger, and I destroyed most of my experiments of that time."

After that, his sculpture began with a relief-like quality only one step removed from the two-dimensionality of his painter colleagues. It moved slowly—still remaining within the Cubist idiom toward giving a total existence to the constructed masses of the Cubist concepts.

Fortunately in 1916, a contact with Léonce Rosenberg, a dealer who represented many of the Cubist painters, provided Lipchitz with the materials and substance he so sorely needed.

In the spring of 1917, he married Berthe Kitrosser, a Bessarabian poetess. Because he wanted a portrait made of himself and his young wife Berthe, he decided to ask Modigliani to paint it and thus help his friend financially. Although Lipchitz himself was often short of funds, he searched for ways to help his fellow artists.

"You know my conditions?" asked Modigliani. "It's ten francs for each sitting plus brandy."

Modigliani came with his sketch pad, set it up against the back of a chair, which served as an easel, put a full bottle of brandy beside him, and began to make preliminary drawings.

"He would draw in a curious way; he would start with the eyes and then rapidly draw in everything around them. A distorted but astounding likeness would always emerge. When he had done a number of preparatory drawings and had finally decided on the way in which he would make the portrait, he brought an old canvas, already painted by somebody, and over the old picture he began to paint. It was one o'clock when he started. By five he announced that he was finished. So quickly? I was amazed. I ran up to see the painting. Indeed, it was finished. But I wanted to pay him more than for just those few sittings. So I said: 'You know, a sculptor likes a little more material.' 'Well,' said Modigliani, 'if you want me to spoil it, I can come back.' "

Lipchitz had him come back to work on the painting every day for two weeks, until he could find no more to criticize.

"I think he never worked that long on one portrait alone," said Lipchitz, amused.

At one time Lipchitz had perhaps fifteen of the preparatory drawings for this portrait by Modigliani but gave almost all of them away. One day, for example, a Russian poet visited him and asked for financial help. Lipchitz told him that he had no money, but said: "Take two of the Modigliani drawings; perhaps you can sell them."

So he gave them away one after another. One of the drawings is now in the Lyman Collection and another in the Metropolitan Museum.

Eventually the portrait, too, changed hands—and wound up in a museum. It came about in this fashion—although Lipchitz' dealer, Léonce Rosenberg, had helped him considerably during the war years, there was no real understanding between the two men.

"He had, of course, my entire production, and among them were two stones which I did not like any more. I asked him if he would let me have them back. But he said: 'I will sell them to you for six thousand francs.' Naturally, I did not have so much money, so I offered him the Modigliani portrait in trade for the two stones, which he accepted. I destroyed the stones. So you see, I lost the two stones and the portrait at the same time. Perhaps today I would not be so critical of the stones, but then I could not stand them."

The Modigliani portrait now hangs in the Chicago Art Institute.

When Lipchitz' sculpture moved away from the abstractions of analytical Cubism toward more representational forms, Rosenberg objected: "You should stay where you were!" Lipchitz, rightfully, resented the interference, and they often quarrelled.

After a very successful one-man exhibition in 1920, through which Lipchitz's work achieved high acclaim, Rosenberg would not show his sculpture in the exhibit rooms any longer but kept it hidden in the back rooms. As a result, Lipchitz decided to free himself of his contract with Rosenberg. His friends helped him buy back his entire production of about four years.

After that, things went badly for Lipchitz. He had no dealer, and very few prospective buyers found their way to his studio in Montparnasse. Soon he had hardly enough money to buy materials and food, and he became deeply depressed and discouraged. What made the situation even worse was that he could not find the inner strength and harmony to work.

Then, as fate sometimes works, a visitor came to his studio—a visitor who was to have a decisive influence on the future course of Lipchitz' life and career.

A Paris art dealer, Paul Guillaume, brought an American to Lipchitz' studio. The stranger did not speak French, but their conversation quickly changed to German and Yiddish. The American seemed to know a great deal about modern art and had very definite opinions. Lipchitz was impressed by his direct manner. He picked out eight sculptures, carefully questioning Lipchitz about the price of each. At first Lipchitz quoted a very low sum, for fear of losing the sale. But with each piece the stranger chose, his courage rose and so did the price. He thought to himself, "This man, whom I don't even know, has chosen my most important works, and I cannot let them go for the mere price of a few meals."

To Lipchitz' astonishment, the stranger offered him only slightly less for the eight pieces than he had asked. The American handed him a card and said: "Please have these pieces sent to me in America; you will receive payment upon receipt."

Lipchitz, still in a daze, glanced at the card—Dr. Alfred Barnes, Merion, Pennsylvania. The name meant nothing to him then—only that this stranger had relieved him of his immediate worries about food and materials.

The next day he received a message from Paul Guillaume, asking him to come to his gallery. Lipchitz arrived at the appointed time and was ushered into a room where Dr. Barnes was waiting for him, surrounded by sketches and drawings of a building. He explained that this was the building he had commissioned to house his immense art collection in Merion, a suburb of Philadelphia, and asked Lipchitz to make him a proposal for several pieces of sculpture to be placed in a number of niches. Characteristic of Barnes, he wanted the proposal and a cost estimate the next day. Lipchitz drew, designed, and figured all night. In the morning he handed his proposal to Barnes, who accepted it.

Lipchitz was overjoyed and exuberant over this sudden stroke of luck. Colleagues and friends who saw him with Dr. Barnes would come up and ask to be introduced to this wealthy American collector who seemed to possess the power of making an artist renowned. Through the ensuing years Lipchitz and Barnes became very good friends.

One summer when they were strolling through the Paris museums and galleries, Barnes expressed a desire to see Soutine's work. Lipchitz took him to his atelier, and Barnes bought a great number of paintings from him. On another occasion they visited Modigliani's former dealer Zborowski, and Barnes, enchanted with the paintings, bought a number of them, thereby initiating Modigliani's international acclaim. Tragically, Modigliani did not live to enjoy his success.

More affluent now and with a feeling of security, Lipchitz purchased some property in the lovely section outside of Paris known as Boulogne-sur-Seine, overlooking the river. He chose a young, then rather unknown architect, Charles Edouard Jeaneret (who called himself Le Corbusier), to design his home and studio. The site of Lipchitz' property along the Seine was ideal for Le Corbusier's architectural designs. The walls and the roof of the structure would protect the man inside from the hostile elements; otherwise, the house was functional, organic, a part of the environment—changing, breathing with both the occupant and the world around it.

In 1925 the house was completed. It was magnificent with its walls of glass, its terraced roof and garden, its sun openings that brought in light and air. Lipchitz' friends thought he was insane to spend so much money, but his new dwelling was so exhilarating in its light and tranquility that he was able to plunge into his work with new energy and fervor. Just as the structure of the house was designed to bring in light and air, Lipchitz became obsessed with the idea of endowing his sculpture with light and air, freeing it from the bonds of its own solidity and massiveness. He started by working on cardboard models punctured with openings. Then came the first bronze, *Pierrot*, which to the amazement of his foundry was successfully cast. He continued to work in the new medium of his transparencies. At last, by penetration of the sheer mass of the sculpture, he had opened it up, articulating solid as well as space and light values. The static rigidity of the solid mass was transformed into a more dynamic sculptural expression in which the "transparent" sculpture became an organic unity with space about it. His sculpture no longer had bounds; it gave the feeling of flight.

Even in the early 1930's Lipchitz could hear the ominous rumblings from within Germany. He sensed the impending terror and doom of the Hitler regime and expressed his feelings in the sculpture *David and Goliath*. On the fallen giant he carved the swastika. Thus his art began to reflect the relation between his inner self and the developments in Europe.

"I was angry and afraid, and also hopeful that tomorrow Hitler would be finished," Lipchitz said. "That is why I made my Goliath this way. It was my prayer."

In 1936 he was commissioned by the French government to make a sculpture for the Palace of Discovery and Inventions at the 1937 World's Fair in Paris. A dream of many years found its fulfillment—to make a monumental work of sculpture.

Lipchitz chose the mythical theme of Prometheus. "Prometheus," he said, "personifies science, fire, medicine—in short, progress. More importantly, Prometheus also represents the struggle between day and night, good and bad, progress and retrogression."

Earlier, in 1933, he had made a small *Prometheus*. But now came his opportunity to create a Prometheus of gigantic dimensions. His was a Prometheus unbound, a Prometheus who had broken the chain and was strangling the vulture. Against darkness and oppression, Prometheus struggles to bring light to man. Prometheus personifies the artist's struggle against the bonds of his art, man's fight against oppression. The magnificent *Prometheus* was for Lipchitz a total work, an answer to his own secret hopes. It was to be thirty feet high and placed forty-five feet above the ground over the entrance gate. This magnificent work was awarded the Gold Medal.

When the World's Fair closed, the sculpture was moved to a garden along the Champs Elysées. But France was torn by political tensions, and certain reactionary elements began to see something subversive in his *Prometheus*. After a bitter campaign in the newspaper *Le Matin, Prometheus* was pulled down and demolished.

Now the rumblings from inside Germany were swelling to a roar. On September 1, 1939, Hitler invaded Poland. Two days later France was at war. In May, 1940, the Battle of France was on.

With the German armies practically at the outskirts of Paris, Lipchitz locked his studio and fled with friends by car, leaving everything behind. Their flight ended in Toulouse, which had been declared a free zone. Lipchitz felt relatively safe there. Friends quickly found a place for him, and to dispel his depression he tried to work again. The sculpture *Flight* was born during those dark, despairing weeks and months.

At the beginning of the war the Louvre encouraged collectors and artists to put their collections in the Museum's cellars. Fortunately, Lipchitz did not comply. He managed to bury some of his pieces in his garden, and others he shipped to southern France. The Germans subsequently burned many of the paintings and art treasures stored in the basement of the Louvre, and Lipchitz's bronzes would surely have been melted down as scrap metal for the production of ammunition.

Almost a year from the day he fled Paris, Lipchitz and Berthe set out across the Atlantic, aboard a small Portuguese vessel, toward America, where they were to remain for the duration of the war.

When Lipchitz returned briefly to France after the war, Paris was no longer the same to him. The war had left its ugly scars on the land and its people, but that was not all that had changed. He had changed, too. America was now what France had become for him in his early youth. After seven months of trying to readjust to life in Paris —seven months of indecision and conflict with himself—he returned to America to stay, bringing with him the courage and stamina which he was going to need to build a new life at the age of 56. His wife Berthe decided to remain in France as a permanent separation.

On his return, early in 1947, he attacked his work with new vigor. He began to make a larger version of *Miracle*, which he had done in France in 1940. This new version represented to him a prayer of grace, of thanksgiving for the sovereignty of Israel. Then followed *Sacrifice II*, *Hagar*, and *Rescue II*.

Despite Lipchitz's departure, France did not forget her famous adopted son. It was a proud and happy moment when he received the Cross of the Legion of Honor, the highest possible honor that France could bestow on him.

In 1948, he met and married Yulla Halberstadt, a refugee from Nazi persecution.

A few months after this marriage, he received a distinguished visitor, Père Couturier. Father Couturier had been a well-known personality around art circles in Paris and an outspoken defender of modern art in churches. He had come especially from Canada to meet Lipchitz and to discuss a proposal, made two years earlier, that Lipchitz sculpture a Virgin for their church in Assy, a small town in the French Alps near the Swiss border.

Lipchitz was extremely pleased with this visit, because ever since Father Couturier's representative had talked to him in Paris he had thought a great deal about this Virgin and had become more and more enthusiastic about the idea. Lipchitz did not wish to be paid for his work. The church would bear only the expense of casting and shipping. Instead of payment Lipchitz requested permission to produce and sell two additional casts of *Notre Dame de Liesse (Our Lady of Joy)*, as he had named her. One of these casts was placed in a shrine at New Harmony, Indiana, and the other in the ancient Abbey of Saint Columba on Iona, a small island in the North Atlantic near the Scottish coast.

Lipchitz spent the entire year of 1951 working on the Virgin for Assy. Then, when she was almost finished and ready to be cast, disaster struck and completely destroyed her.

"It happened on a Saturday—January 5, 1952. I was at home with my family. Around seven o'clock in the evening the police called and told me that my studio on Washington Square had burned out. I left immediately and came downtown, but they would not let me go up to my studio on the fifth floor because it was too dark and very dangerous. So I went home, and as soon as it was light again I came back and I found only a hole in the ground. My statues were sticking out of the ashes; they found some of my things in the basement. I lost a tremendous amount of work. At least ten years of my work here in New York was destroyed as well as a lot of my collection which I had brought over from France. I was finished, absolutely ruined! For two weeks I could not get over the shock. But then I began to work again, and I am still working, so now I am all right."

The fire had started in the early morning hours, caused by a short circuit in a painter's studio on the floor below Lipchitz', and had raged through the building. All of Lipchitz' drawings and sketches were burned. His valuable art collection, recovered from the war, had perished in the flames—Soutine, Cézanne, Gris, Picasso, African art objects. Almost everything else was ruined by water or from ceilings and walls caving in. Many of his plaster models were damaged in this way, broken into a thousand little pieces. Among them was the almost finished plaster of *Notre Dame de Liesse*.

After two terrible weeks, he slowly started to work again. Through the newspapers the American public heard of Lipchitz' loss and the spontaneous reaction was overwhelming. Letters came in from all over the country, many of them with money or checks enclosed. Lipchitz was deeply touched, but he did not want charity. He answered all the letters and returned the money and checks.

Friends stepped in to help; some of them commissioned portraits, others helped organize a committee in collaboration with the Museum of Modern Art to collect funds for a new studio, which he repaid with sculpture. Within a short time enough money had been raised to purchase land near his home in Hastings-on-Hudson, and soon the new building was being erected.

In the meantime, while the new studio was being built, John Spring, owner of the Modern Art Foundry, offered him working space in the foundry. This meant several hours' traveling time from his home to Long Island and back. Yet nothing could keep Lipchitz from his work. Work was the only panacea. Through it he was able to surmount his loss and eventually to turn it into a blessing.

One of the first sculptures that emerged from his hands after the fire was a vision he had seen in the smoldering ruins of his studio—*Virgin in Flames*. Then came *Lesson of a Disaster*.

Working on a new model for *Notre Dame de Liesse*, he suddenly became inspired by an old chisel with a broken wooden handle. He sent several of his chisels to the foundry to be cast in wax. To the wax chisels he added arms and legs, combined figures, and then cast them in bronze.

His imagination created *Variations on a Chisel*, a lighthearted series of bronze figures with various rhythms, twenty-six in all, and each made in a single working day. Sculpturally they are as gay and charming as Beethoven's composition often called *Rage over the Lost Penny* is musically.

On April 12, 1953, Jacques Lipchitz moved into his new studio on the Hudson, and all his friends came to help him celebrate this festive occasion.

Now his spirits and his physical strength were stepped up by the desire to restore all that had been lost in the fire. In 1954 he completed *Notre Dame de Liesse*, and in 1955 she took her place in the church of Assy among the works of other great artists of our time —Chagall, Braque, Léger, and Rouault.

A commission he had received in 1951 for a sculpture for Fairmount Park of the Philadelphia Museum of Fine Arts now absorbed him completely. *The Spirit of Enterprise* which, too, had perished in the fire is a monumental and gigantic work, almost as large as his *Prometheus* for the World's Fair in Paris.

Feverishly he continued to work on the restoration and recasting of a great many sculptures that were destroyed or damaged in the fire of 1952. He has never resigned himself to the fact that the fire was a loss in every respect, for he feels that it purified his vision of the Virgin, *Notre Dame de Liesse*, and clarified his composition for *Spirit of Enterprise*, to mention only a few. A dream he had had ever since he left Paris was at last realized—to work and create in a beautiful, spacious studio.

Suddenly a serious illness laid him up for several months in 1959. For awhile everyone around him doubted that he would ever be strong enough to lift a hammer and start pounding at his bronzes again. After almost a year of slow recovery, however, he regained his strength and at the age of 70 returned to his work with the old vigor.

It is apparent that there will never be an end to his inexhaustible creativity as long as he draws a breath of life.

LA JOIE de VIVRE

Early on a bright spring morning in 1960 I arrived at the home of Jacques Lipchitz, on the edge of the picturesque town of Hastings-on-Hudson, New York. His big white house is situated on a steep, wooded hill overlooking the Hudson as far as the Palisades on the New Jersey side. Gray flagstone steps lead up to the house, which is set back a little in a partly cultivated garden. To the left is a glass-enclosed wing, and to the right one can see some of his sculptures peering through the trees.

We had made this appointment to go to the foundry together—a custom that Lipchitz follows three or four times a week. This was to be our first day together.

I could not help feeling a certain anxiety about the task that lay ahead of me in attempting to render a true and lasting portrait of Jacques Lipchitz—the artist and the man—through my photographs. Sculpture is an art which demands affirmation and avowal. It is a progression of massively perceived shapes and forms. The artist takes a piece of his own reality, the world in which he lives, and frees it from the contingencies of reality. He takes an idea, a part of his inner self—his imagination—and translates it into the three-dimensional reality of his work. To capture and express not only the physical characteristics of the artist but the variety of his creative temperament is no easy task.

What also concerned me was knowing that it would be quite impossible to find access to his work in its entirety. Lipchitz has been a sculptor for more than fifty years and his sculptures are widely scattered over the world.

Going up to the house, I rang the doorbell but there was no response. The house seemed to be deserted.

As I stood on the steps in front of the entrance, undecided what to do next, I noticed an object coming slowly around the corner—I saw a black stick with a limp snake hanging from it. Finally, Lipchitz appeared at the other end of the stick, completely absorbed in his activity. Although I stood only a few steps away from him, he passed right by me, not looking up. I could hear him murmur: "What a pity I had to kill this beautiful creature."

He dropped the snake into a basket and disappeared into the house. Now I was certain he had forgotten our appointment.

But a few seconds later the front door swung open. "Good morning, my friend," he said, smiling, his arms stretched out in cordial greeting. "How are you today?"

He was a changed person. As if to excuse his appearance in the garden, he explained: "You know, I feel so terrible that I had to kill that beautiful animal because of the Little One, my daughter, you know."

Obviously, he had been quite upset. Yet overriding this was the importance of a proper and dignified greeting.

Although Jacques Lipchitz is almost seventy-five years old, he does not look over sixty. His husky body is as unbent and lithe as that of a young athlete, with strong, forceful muscles. Meeting him for the first time, one immediately falls under the spell of his eyes. They are always observing, penetrating. They not only look at you; they look into you, searching out the true human being. His voice is deep and full of warmth, with a distinct French accent. When he speaks he radiates authority and conviction, whether he speaks of his sculptures, of art in general, or of his rich life philosophy. Yet he loves to laugh, and his eyes take on an impish gleam when he does.

Driving down to New York, en route to the foundry, we discussed this and that, carefully feeling each other out. Sensing my anxiety, he immediately put me at ease by chatting and joking. I had met him before—although very briefly. Now I was completely taken by his uncomplicated nature and simplicity of manner. There, sitting beside me, was one of the great sculptors of our time who had, with Picasso and a few of their contemporaries, revolutionized modern art half a century ago and had, in effect, greatly influenced not only art but architecture, design, and other visual fields.

The foundry is located in a desolate part of Long Island. The big, sooty building stands on a dead-end street, looking like any other industrial plant except for the large white letters on its front—MODERN ART FOUNDRY. Its only other distinction is an iron gate.

Lipchitz rang the bell and someone from the office opened the door to let us in. After a cordial "Hello," he marched through the entrance hall and into a room at the opposite end. At first glance this room seemed dark and crowded. A window at the left gave only sparse light, but I could distinguish countless white figures and I realized that we were in the plaster room, where the plaster models are stored before and after casting. It is one of

"He began to work on the wax cast of Joie de Vivre . . ."

the most fascinating places in the foundry. Some sculptures seemed to reach out of the dark; others seemed to embrace. Among old monuments covered with thick layers of dust, I discovered well-known acquaintances. Archipenko's *Boxer,* Lachaisse's *Nude,* and of course the many Lipchitz plasters that have been cast in bronze at the Modern Art Foundry through the years. Looking around this room is like turning the pages of an art book. It houses the past and the present, and even allows glimpses into the future.

The plaster room also serves as a dressing room for Lipchitz; he keeps his working clothes there. One of the workmen came in, bidding him a cheerful "Good morning." Noticing my cameras, he turned to Lipchitz.

"Well, Jacques, now that you are being photographed you'll have to get yourself some fancy new clothes for around here."

Lipchitz laughed and shrugged: "Why should I get new clothes when they will be the same in a few days?" Beside him were his wax- and plaster-drenched working pants.

He took me on a tour of the foundry, greeting everybody with a hearty "Good morning." I could plainly see from the expressions on the men's faces how glad they were to see him, how well liked he is. He considers himself as part of the big, happy family. Seeing him in these surroundings, joking, chatting, and giving a friendly pat to the faithful old watchdog, it is hard to realize that this is the master, Jacques Lipchitz.

The foundry is like an international melting pot. There are many nationalities represented among the workers—Russian, Polish, Italian, German, French, American. With each of the men Lipchitz usually speaks in his native tongue, particularly if he has to criticize or scold one of them. Needless to say, he demands the utmost not only from the men but also from himself. His disarming sense of humor, however, never fails to disperse any disagreement quickly.

Adjoining the plaster room is the furnace room, the heart of the foundry, where the roaring fire burns day and night. Through this room we walked to an adjacent building, actually a huge studio, where Lipchitz occupies a corner when working in the foundry. The rest of the room is used for preparing the wax models for casting.

In his studio at the foundry Lipchitz is the master again. He began to work on the wax cast of *Joie de Vivre (Joy of Life),* a large rhythmical sculpture which Vicomte Charles de Noailles commissioned in 1927 for the garden of his villa at Hyères in southern France. It is a significant work because it was the first transparency which Lipchitz executed on a monumental scale. *Joie de Vivre* is sculptured in a bold, architectonic manner. It represents a dancing figure with a big musical instrument. Silhouetted against the sky, it gives the illusion of motion. When the sculpture was first exhibited in Paris it bore the inscription, *J'aime le mouvement qui déplace les formes.*

While heating his tools on the gas burner for working with the wax, Lipchitz explained his concern with movement for the first issue of *Joie de Vivre:*

"The Vicomte's villa was on a hill, and from the terrace you could not see all the aspects of the statue. In order to show the statue from all angles I put machinery inside the pedestal so that it would make one revolution every four minutes; and from many points of the house, the terrace, and the garden one could, with a switch, make the statue turn or stop. It was the first turning statue up to that time. It was, I thought, something new in France. But I will tell you a story about that. While I was working on the statue, a peasant from around there came to me and said, 'You Parisian, you think that you are the first one to make a turning statue? You are wrong. We have a turning statue here in our church, a Virgin, and it was made in the fourteenth century. She was made to help people in distress on the sea. If a disaster is announced, we turn the Virgin in that direction so that she will save the people.' So, you see, I only *thought* that this was the first turning sculpture."

The lost wax process—the seams are removed.

Metal pins are inserted to give support.

It is not at all unusual that Lipchitz now casts an early work such as *Joie de Vivre*. This particular issue he made for an upcoming retrospective exhibition.

To make bronze casts is a costly undertaking, and in his early years Lipchitz often did not have the means or the time to make casts of every sculpture. Besides, many casts were lost or destroyed through two wars and other destructive events, and these have to be recast for exhibitions and acquisitions. This retrospective activity gives Lipchitz great pleasure and satisfaction. He makes as many as seven issues of one sculpture, but no more. Each cast or issue is signed and numbered and bears his fingerprint next to the issue number.

Setting up my cameras that first morning in the foundry, I felt his eyes following me as he continued to work on his statue. Yet he never interfered, never told me what to do or what not to do. In the same fashion I never asked him to do anything for me or pose for me. All photographs, including the portraits, were taken as the situation occurred. When I

Gates and vents are fastened to the cast.   *Heat-resistant plaster is poured around the wax.*

noticed that my lights annoyed him, I quickly turned them off and never again used artificial light. Everything was photographed in available light.

The procedure of bronze casting that Lipchitz follows is an ancient one called *cire
perdue*, or the lost wax process. Michelangelo, Benvenuto Cellini, and many other great
sculptors used it.

From the final plaster cast a negative is made in two sections of a gelatinlike substance.
This is supported by an outer plaster covering, and several layers of beeswax are brushed
over it. Then the sections are carefully placed together, and wax at a low temperature is
poured inside the negative. The wax remains inside until the outer surfaces harden to the
desired thickness, which will later determine the thickness of the bronze. Excess wax is
poured out and the negative mold is removed, leaving a hollow wax replica of the sculpture which now has to be retouched.

With keen interest, Lipchitz watches the white metal flow out of the furnace.

Under his supervision, the bronze is poured into the mold.

Unlike most sculptors, Lipchitz always retouches the wax casts himself rather than having the foundry do it.

"Every time I retouch a wax," he explains, "from day to day I am in a different mood. I see and want to express different textures and details. Even though I make as many as seven casts of one sculpture, each issue will be different in small details. I don't wish them to be identical."

By reworking the wax of *Joie de Vivre* with a hot iron, Lipchitz adds life and excitement to the broad surfaces. The texture must be restored. The seams and imperfections caused by the wax casting have to be smoothed out. With pliable beeswax he painstakingly goes over the entire sculpture, preparing it for casting in bronze.

A network of gates and vents in the form of wax rods is now fastened to the wax cast. This is necessary for the entrance of bronze and the subsequent escape of air during the pouring of the bronze. Then heat-resistant plaster is poured around the wax, forming a mold, with the ends of the gates and vents still exposed. The inside of the wax cast is also

Lipchitz reworking the bronze surface of Joie de Vivre, *1927, 7¼' high.*

filled with plaster. After these preparations, the mold is baked over a slow fire to melt the wax inside—hence the name "lost wax." The liquid wax runs out through the vents and gates, a slow process which may take two or three days for a large sculpture such as *Joie de Vivre*. After all the wax has melted and drained, the plaster mold is placed in a sand pit. It is now ready for the bronze to be poured into the space from which the wax was "lost."

Despite the fact that the melting and pouring of metal is a daily routine at the foundry, it never ceases to be a thrilling moment for artist and workmen alike. The air is filled with tension and anticipation. It is a delicate task, and the men perform their jobs with intense concentration, signaling one another only with a glance or the stir of a hand.

Lipchitz was standing near the forge, watching the blazing white metal flow out of the furnace. Following the men who carried the hot metal, he supervised the pouring of the bronze into the mold. In a matter of seconds the job was finished and everybody sighed with relief. But Lipchitz did not relax. His anxiety is almost proverbial and does not cease until the bronze has cooled, the plaster has been removed from around and inside, and he assures himself that the cast has turned out perfectly.

SPIRIT OF ENTERPRISE

The working model of Spirit of Enterprise *is used in planning the casting.*

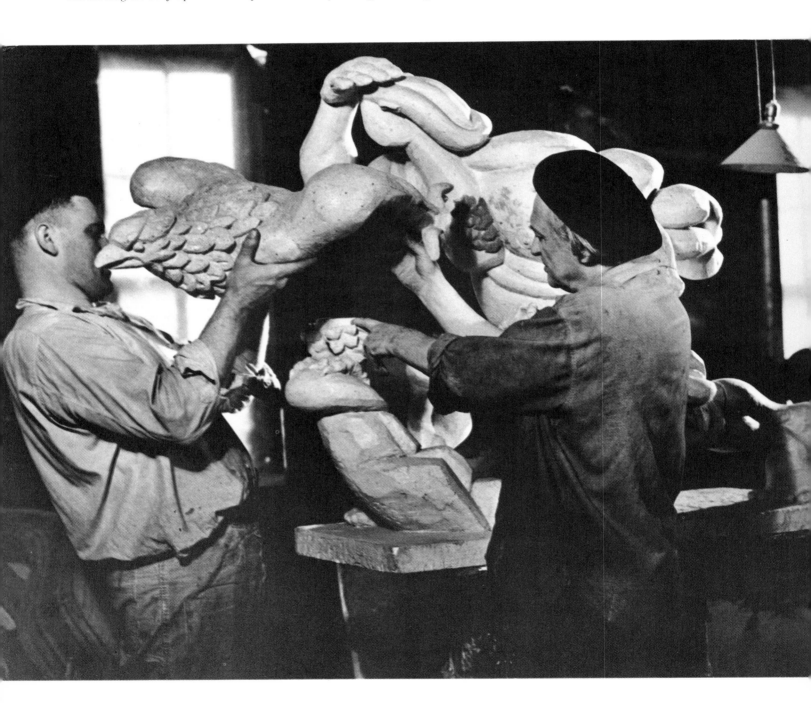

Ever since the unhappy experiences with his two versions of *Prometheus*—the first having been demolished by reactionaries in Paris and the other misrepresented in Brazil—Lipchitz yearned for another opportunity to make a monumental and symbolic work which would in some manner cap the endeavors of his life. The commission he received in 1951 from the Fairmount Art Committee to make a statue entitled *The Constructive Enterprise* was the answer to his hopes. The sculpture was proposed for a terrace in Fairmount Park in Philadelphia. Lipchitz felt that the suggested title was not appropriate and asked the Committee to change it to *The Spirit of Enterprise*, which they accepted.

He began to make numerous sketches and studies, introducing an eagle into the composition as the symbol of America's progressive tendencies and power. He found, however, that there would not be sufficient room on the terrace for the massive sculpture he had in mind, because the Committee had planned to place a sculpture by Sir Jacob Epstein alongside the Lipchitz statue. Then the model he had prepared was completely destroyed by the disastrous fire in his Washington Square studio in January 1952.

Small imperfections which occur during the final casting are corrected by the sculptor.

When Lipchitz recovered from the shock of the fire, he courageously started to create a new *Spirit of Enterprise,* slightly modified in concept. At this time the Fairmount Art Committee decided to designate another site for the Epstein statue, inasmuch as he, too, had submitted sketches for a large piece of sculpture. Now Lipchitz was free to put emphasis on the American eagle which he wanted initially, and thereby clarify his composition.

His conception of a young man peering ahead with one hand on his forehead as if overlooking this great land of opportunities, and with the other hand holding a caduceus guided by the eagle, is his interpretation of America's proficiency and vast energy in the fields of science, commerce, and the arts. The powerful work conveys a sense of great force in arrested motion, as if the entire sculpture holding itself back for a moment—about to set off for new and greater enterprise.

Details of the final cast are compared with the working model.

When I first met Lipchitz and, a short time later, began the photographs for this book, *The Spirit of Enterprise* was just being cast, a process that took more than a year. Because of its gigantic dimensions—twelve feet high and sixteen feet long—it was necessary to cast it in twenty separate sections which later were assembled, screwed, and welded together into one harmonious unit weighing nine tons.

While most sculptors depend entirely on the services of their foundry, Lipchitz takes great pride in working along with the foundrymen. With a keen eye he supervises and follows every step of the operations. To him this is an important part of the creative evolution that is taking place.

He moves about with the calm self-assurance of a man who is master of his actions and his creations. His more than fifty years of experience in every phase of casting make him an expert who can give counsel to the men working in the foundry and whose opinion is highly respected by all.

It is always a thrilling moment when a sculpture is being assembled, section by section, gradually becoming a reality. It is a moment of truth for the artist, like a father seeing

his newborn child for the first time. Even in the reduced model or the enlargement it is not always possible to envision the full impact of a sculpture. Up to the moment of assembly the vision has existed primarily in the artist's imagination, but now he is confronted with the final result of his endeavors.

Constantly comparing various details of the bronze cast with the smaller working model, he is using the working model as an ideal for the final work. He becomes inspired by the play of light on his bronze and makes limited changes accordingly.

He even climbs inside the bronze and, with ear-splitting noise, hammers out specific sections. Then he climbs on top and around it, examining every inch of the huge sculpture, hammering, filing, and polishing with great care. As precisely and carefully as the foundry workers operate, small imperfections do appear during casting and have to be corrected. Lipchitz has developed a sharp eye for them.

Just watching him is enough to exhaust a much younger man. Yet Lipchitz has the endurance of a giant as he performs this arduous and painstaking task of putting the finishing touches on one of his sculptures.

Spirit of Enterprise, 1960, bronze, 12′ 1″ x 16′ 1″, Fairmount Park, Philadelphia Museum of Fine Arts.

44

PEGASUS

To the finished bronze of *Pegasus* Lipchitz applies the patina, which is a forced coating of the corrosion of copper or copper-rich metal such as bronze. In ancient times, sculptures were buried in the soil for many years so that a natural incrustation would form on the metal. Depending on the compound of chemicals and acids in the metal as well as in the soil in which the sculpture was buried, a large variety of shades—greens, reds, blacks, blues—could be obtained. Also exposure to the weather will slowly form a natural patina on the metal.

The application of artificial patinas has been practiced for centuries, with a variety of "secret" formulas. Apart from its artistic effects, the patina has a practical side—it is a durable, protective coating for the virgin metal.

Lipchitz's habit of applying the patina himself is again unique. Customarily sculptors have this done by the foundry. He, however, selects the many different shades of patina, like a painter, giving his sculpture its final touch of perfection before sending it off to an exhibition, a museum, or a collector.

The blowtorch flame produces the chemical reaction that makes the patina.

Nimbly he moves about the sculpture, dabbing it with a sponge that is saturated in his own secret mixture of metal oxides, brushing the metal with the flame of a blowtorch and washing off excess chemicals, thereby burning in the hot patina. When the flame leaps up and licks around the chemically treated metal, a rainbow of colorful sparks showers down. It is a time-consuming process, but absolute perfection is the result. There are a number of other processes for giving patina to the metal, but they are all more mechanized and less creative.

Lipchitz is usually so engrossed in his activity that he forgets the time of day. For hours he stands there, not resting until the task is completed.

Pegasus, the old fable tells us, was the mythical horse that gave birth to the Muses by striking his hoof on a rock of Mount Olympus. This theme inspired Lipchitz again, some time later, to make *Birth of the Muses*, a much larger version of the Greek myth.

Pegasus, *1944, bronze, 20" high.*

AWAY FROM THE STUDIO

At the Guggenheim museum in New York.

After the strenuous work at the foundry Lipchitz likes to go into Manhattan and visit art galleries, antique shops, and museums. It is both relaxing and recreational for him, as important a phase of his daily schedule as are his trips to the foundry.

Customarily he likes to stop for lunch at a small Greek restaurant on 34th Street, where he has been going for many years. Here the continental atmosphere, the food, music, and people all remind him of Europe and Paris. He has great nostalgia for Paris. Throughout New York he searches out and regularly visits places that remind him of the city of his artistic development and maturing. Although he completely accepts and loves New York, he has transferred many of the places of his affection in Paris to places in New York—

52

Personage, 1916, stone, 43¾" high.

Hastings-on-Hudson has become his Boulogne-sur-Seine; the little Greek restaurant, a café on the rue du Montparnasse. Visits to the Third Avenue antique shops recall his visits to the Flea Market during his Paris decades.

Against the background of towering buildings, along noisy streets teeming with mechanized contrivances, Lipchitz walks as if he is searching for green trees and open spaces. He claims bewilderment with anything mechanical:

"About mechanical things I know nothing. I have a lot of difficulty when I want to play the stereo, you know. I love music, but when the record is finished I don't know how to turn it off. The Little One taught me, but I forget, and now when the record is over I have to yell, 'Please come and help me.' "

It is astonishing that for all his attempts to escape mechanization he has chosen to live and work near New York, which is probably one of the most mechanized cities in the world.

At the Greek restaurant one day we met Isadore Grossman, his former assistant, and we had lunch together. Grossman reminded him of the time when they went to see the Patterson-Johannsen fight. With amusement in his voice Lipchitz recalled:

"You know, when I told my framers, who are wonderful and charming people, that I went to the fights, they were shocked and said: 'But Mr. Lipchitz, the fights are so brutal.' I said, 'Fighting is not brutal, it is beautiful. It is like a good drawing, you see. In order to make a good drawing you have to have the same things that you need for a good fight—craftsmanship, talent, intelligence, and, most importantly, speed. Only, if you make a bad drawing, nothing will happen to you. But if you give a bad fight you will be hit hard and you will be knocked out.' It was a beautiful fight. I saw it all very well with my binoculars."

Galleries, museums, a favorite neighborhood restaurant, and walks through the city's streets
afford relaxation and impressions that become an integral part of the artist's life.

After lunch we often wandered together through antique shops, museums, and art galleries.

"Ah, this is a beautiful piece," he would say, admiring a Hindu sculpture or an African carving. "I am looking at it with envy, because I cannot afford to have it. It is too expensive for me." Later when I visited him at home I often found the pieces he had admired so much but "could not afford."

About his deep interest in primitive art he explained:

"We are not newborn babies in this world, we are a continuation of millions of generations of human beings. It is good to know what human beings before us have done in order that we may learn how to proceed. It gives me strength. This is the main ideal by which I am guided in collecting art. I am not so attracted by what you now call beauty; it is for me only a small part of that. But thinking what it means and how it was done is important to me. In this spirit I collect art of all times, primitive art especially but not exclusively.

"We live in such an era, a point of development which causes us to better understand primitive art. We are at the beginning of a new cycle. We have discovered the entire globe and we learn about people on different parts of the globe. Therefore, primitive art means more to us now. It is a universal language, communicating to us the desires, hopes, and endeavors of ancient man and time."

One day when we were both tired from walking around, I suggested that we stop for refreshments at a nearby coffee shop. Around a small table, in the hazy light of the late afternoon, we sat silently for some time. Lipchitz was intensely alert and curiously watching through the window the movements and expressions of the people passing by in the crowd. Absorbed in his thoughts, he picked up a conversation which he had interrupted earlier:

"You know, my generation always felt that we were at a crossroad. We were dissatisfied with the Impressionists and the things that were made after nature. We felt strongly that this was not enough, and our generation wanted to build their own art with the elements of their imagination. Imagination is a very precise thing, you know — it is not fantasy. Remember, the other day I gave you the example of what I mean, what the difference between fantasy and imagination is. I gave you the example of the man who invented the wheel while he was observing another man walking. That is imagination! To do something which just comes to your mind, without any purpose — well, that's fantasy. That also is very interesting, it can be very rich and lovely, but it is not imagination. Imagination comes to precise results and these results are wanted from the beginning. Often imagination and fantasy are confused with one another, or misunderstood."

The waiter had walked up during the last part of Lipchitz's explanation, seemingly listening to our conversation but actually just waiting to take our order. When Lipchitz had finished, the waiter asked, glancing at our plaster-specked shoes: "You guys must be in the construction business?" I quickly answered in a joking tone: "That's right. He"—pointing to Lipchitz—"works for me."

Lipchitz grinned, and the waiter disappeared, obviously confused. We looked at each other and laughed.

One day a woman came to his studio, wanting to buy a piece of sculpture. After looking around, she stopped in front of a large bronze and asked: "Mr. Lipchitz, how do you manage to drill these holes?" — pointing at the openings in one of the transparencies.

"She was like a savage," he said scornfully. "I immediately decided not to sell her anything. You understand? An artist must be very careful and concerned where he places his work. I feel like a protective father to my things. You see, it is not only the artist who must have imagination, but the collector, the initial buyer must have it too."

The woman continued to look around. Then she pointed to a piece and asked the price of it. He quoted a sum he knew was quite high, because he wanted to discourage her from buying. At this moment his little daughter Lolya, then only about seven years old,

came into the studio and heard the price he had quoted the woman. She pulled her father aside into a corner and whispered: "But, Papa, that is too much money." "Well then, how much do you think I should ask?" She thought for a moment and said: "Perhaps three dollars?"

Lipchitz chuckled in amusement, remembering this episode.

Back in the car and on our way home I asked him if he hoped that his daughter would become an artist.

"She is not interested as yet," he replied. "Besides, I would not like her to become an artist—it is a very hard and difficult life. For me, I would not want to be anything else—I could not be! But being her father, I would not want her to have such a hard life."

As we walked up the steps to his house, I noticed for the first time *Joie de Vivre* in the garden to the right of the house. He explained that it had been installed just recently. This dancing figure could not have been placed more eloquently among the wild flowers, bushes, and trees. The garden stretches far up the hill and many other sculptures dominate this natural environment.

Inside the house, the walls of the spacious rooms are adorned with his immense collection of paintings, water colors, and drawings by Manet, Bonnard, Soutine, Gericault,

Cézanne, Kandinsky, Ensor, Goya, Renoir, Degas, Ingres, Pissaro. I was overwhelmed not only by the enormous quantity but also by their quality. In his bedroom, where countless framed and unframed canvases are stacked against the wall for lack of hanging space, my eye was caught by a magnificent Cubist water color by Picasso, and Lipchitz recalled when he got it:

"Picasso asked me one day to pick a work that I particularly liked. I picked this one. Afterward I felt a little guilty. I remember that I said to him, 'You know, I picked the best one,' and I apologized for it. But he answered, 'That's what I wanted you to do.' I treasure this water color very much."

Mingling with art objects of many centuries are his own sculptures. To take care of the overflow he built a glass-enclosed wing, his own private gallery.

The hours at home he spends in relaxation—reading, writing, listening to music with Yulla, his beautiful and exotic wife, and Lolya, their blossoming teen-age daughter, or entertaining a small circle of friends.

"I am a solitary man," he says. "I don't like to travel. But in my house, my rooms, I have the entire humanity around me from ancient times through the present time. Therefore I don't ever feel lonely. I feel that I am part of humanity through it, a link in the eternal evolution."

"*. . . in my house, my rooms, I have the entire humanity around me . . .*"

In Lipchitz' home gallery—Sacrifice II, 1948-1952, bronze, 49¼" high.

NOTRE DAME de LIESSE

Lipchitz with his wife Yulla and daughter Lolya.

There are no windows looking out on the Hudson River in Lipchitz's studio.

"If I could see this magnificent scenery," he explained, "I would probably never work. I would be looking out there for hours watching the boats coming in, and every time I would see a ship outward bound my thoughts would sail away with it."

The studio, a huge, modern, two-story building with two wings, is located just a few minutes from his home. It is filled with pieces of sculpture and models. Seeing it for the first time, I thought of the overwhelming number of sculptures Lipchitz has made in his lifetime. I was filled with awe that one human being alone had created such eloquent work. A stroke of luck had placed before me a large portion of his life's work, just re-turned from a two-year exhibition tour of Europe—Stedelijk Museum, Amsterdam; Rijk-museum Kroller-Muller, Otterlo; and the museums of Basel, Dortmund, Paris, Brussels, and London.

When I arrived one day at the studio, he mentioned casually that more than a hun-dred pieces of sculpture had been picked up for an exhibit. I looked around, expecting to find a bare spot, but the studio looked as overflowing as ever. It always amazed me that he could find certain things among the seeming disorder of plasters, bronzes, models, sketches, and the like. Whenever I asked him for a specific piece, he would walk directly to where it was, sometimes buried under drawings.

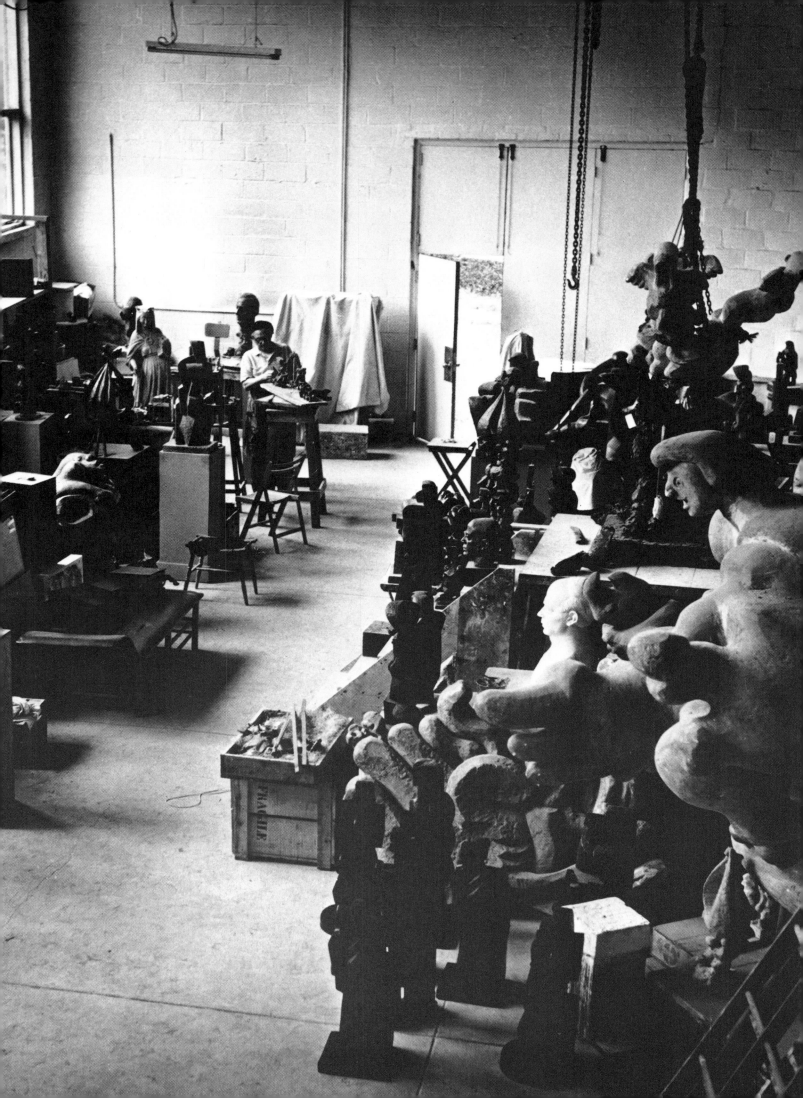

In the studio I usually worked at the opposite end from where he was. For hours sometimes there was complete silence, as if the white plasters were absorbing all sounds. Occasionally, when the door is open and the sunlight streams in, you can hear the cheerful twittering of the birds. Lipchitz loves this peace and quiet. He needs it to be in undisturbed unity with his creative imagination.

Rarely does he sit down while working. But when he worked on the model for the gate of the shrine at New Harmony, Indiana, he had to sit down in order to conceive the proper perspective from which the top part of the gate would be seen in reality. The finished gate is seventeen feet high.

His eyes and his hands always work in unity; they are never separated, which is clearly seen in his concentrated expression. By the time he lifts his tools and approaches a theme, every movement is definite and without hesitation. His hands are merely the obedient tools of his mind, and his eyes are the judge.

Model for the gate of the shrine at New Harmony.

By looking up at the model, Lipchitz checks the perspective as it will appear to the viewer of the finished gate.

The finished gate.

Notre Dame de Liesse, 1948-1953, bronze, 75″ high, New Harmony, Indiana.

One day he told how his sculpture *Notre Dame de Liesse* came into being:

"When I was at my exhibition at the Gallery Maeght in Paris in 1946, a Dominican priest approached me. He introduced himself as representative of Père Couturier, a well-known designer of stained-glass windows and also a Dominican priest. He asked me if I might be willing to make a Virgin for their church at Assy. 'Do you think that I can make such a thing?' I asked. 'We know everything about you and your work,' he replied, 'and we would very much like to have you make a Virgin for our church.' 'But do you know that I am a Jew?' He said: 'Well, if this does not disturb you, it certainly does not disturb us.' I liked this answer so much that I accepted without hesitation, and he said that he would get in touch with me again later."

When Father Couturier himself visited Lipchitz in 1948 to discuss this Virgin for the church of Notre Dame de Toute Grace, at Assy, a small mountain village near the

The shrine at New Harmony.

At night, concealed lighting points up the detail of Notre Dame de Liesse.

Swiss border, Lipchitz explained that he had only one condition in making this Virgin—
he wished her to bear the following inscription:

*Jacob Lipchitz, Juif, fidèle à la foi de ses ancetres, a fait cette vierge pour la
bonne entente des hommes sur la terre, afin que l'espirt règne.*

*Jacob Lipchitz (his biblical name), Jew, faithful to the religion of his ancestors,
has made this Virgin for better understanding among all people of this earth,
so that the spirit may prevail.*

Father Couturier did not react immediately. Thoughtfully he folded the piece of
paper on which Lipchitz had written the inscription and said that he would have to con-
sult with his superiors. For several months Lipchitz waited for an answer. Then one day
he received a glowing letter commending him on his inscription and accepting it.

Lipchitz started to make preliminary sketches immediately, but was utterly dissatisfied. Nothing came—nothing was right. For weeks he tormented himself in an effort to
envision the Virgin. The inspiration came when he learned of his wife's hopeful condition—he was to become a father! This would be his first child, the fulfillment of a long-
cherished wish. Jubilant and filled with thanks, his heart and his hands formed the Virgin.

Five studies for Notre Dame de Liesse, *8½" to 10½" high.*

The study for Notre Dame de Liesse, *1948, bronze, 33″ high.*

Study for Between Heaven and Earth, *1958, bronze, 46" high.*

Work on Between Heaven and Earth, *a continuation from* Notre Dame de Liesse, *was started in 1960.*

He enclosed her in a canopied heart resting on the backs of cherubims and held together on top by the beak of a dove. He called her *Notre Dame de Liesse (Our Lady of Joy)*.

Originally she was to be part of a baptismal font, but the design was later changed, making it possible for Lipchitz to free his composition from all limitations.

Under the agreement that he had made with Father Couturier he wanted no money but asked permission to make and sell two additional casts so that he would be reimbursed for his time and production costs. One cast of *Notre Dame de Liesse* stands on the island of Iona, near the Scottish coast, and the other was bought by Mrs. Jane Owen, who built a shrine at New Harmony, Indiana, in memory of George Rapp and Robert Owen, founders of one of the first Utopian communities in the United States.

George Rapp, a German Pietist preacher, established a prosperous and devout trading community and introduced to America many new and revolutionary ideals, among them a strong educational system based on the Pestalozzi principles.

When Robert Owen, a wealthy philanthropist and reformer, purchased the community in 1825, he renamed it New Harmony. Through his leadership he brought science, free education, and culture to the flourishing town in the Middle West. Jane Owen, wife of one of the descendants of Robert Owen, devoted herself to rebuilding the community along the Wabash River, and dedicated a beautiful shrine to the memory of the two visionary pioneers. Most appropriate to the spirit, she purchased the third cast of *Notre Dame de Liesse*.

After his daughter Lolya was born, Lipchitz expressed his joy and gratitude by making solid silver casts of several different sketches of the Virgin and gave them to his wife Yulla.

Since its inception, *Notre Dame de Liesse* has gone through countless changes. Lipchitz explained how one of these changes came about:

"One day, while working on my Virgin, the bronze cast was in the air, suspended by a crane. I suddenly felt that it would be good to continue the statue at the bottom. I started to make sketches as I saw her, suspended. I call this version *Between Heaven and Earth*. It is not really a biblical theme any more."

The artist at work on the plaster cast of Between Heaven and Earth, *130″ high.*

With a variety of tools the finishing touches are put on the plaster
of Between Heaven and Earth. *Now the work is ready for the foundry.*

STYLE DEVELOPMENT

*At left—*Danseuse Espagnole, *1914, plaster, 27½" high.*
*At right—*Danseuse, *1913, plaster, 27" high.*

Pregnant Woman, *1912, plaster, 25" high.*

Examining the sculptures that Lipchitz has made through the years, one finds it interesting to trace the variation in style from his early beginnings. The elements that have become a part of his sculpturing skills and his themes have merged with his time in an unbroken continuity, resulting in what the name Jacques Lipchitz now means to us and to art history in general.

"I have never made a jump in my career," Lipchitz told me. "One sculpture evolved from the other. Just look around you and see, for instance, here—from my earliest years, 1912 through 1925."

He pointed out an early *Nude* of 1912 standing side by side with *Bather* of 1913. Then he pointed to *Matador* of 1914 and *Dancer* of 1915. The latter is one of his detach-

Matador,
1914, bronze.
31¾" high.

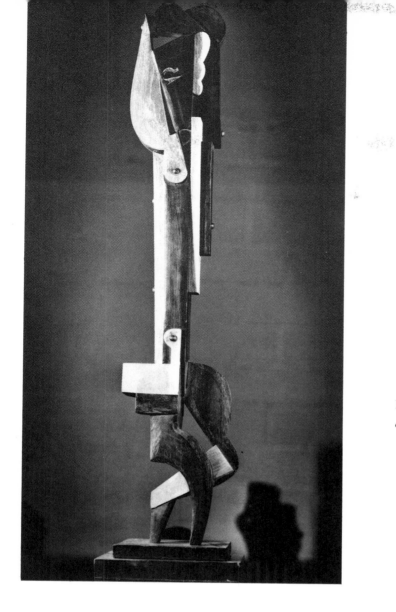

Dancer, *1915, ebony and oak,*
demountable sculpture, 39¼″ high.

able sculptures, made of ebony and oak wood. Then he walked over to *Bather III*, a Cubist work of 1917, and *Woman with Book* of 1919, to his *Seated Man* of 1922, and finally stopped in front of *Pierrot* of 1925, one of his transparencies.

"If you want to continue this style development," he said, "just observe my many versions of *Mother and Child* which have occupied me all through my life, from the earliest one of 1913 up to my last version of 1949. There you have combined in one theme all the styles in which I have ever worked. You will find no abrupt changes when you follow them successively. It is a natural, gradual development — like a child growing into adulthood. Whenever you think you might take a jump ahead, I assure you that it will catch up with you later. It is hard work, but nature does not permit us to make jumps. Nature does not work that way, and therefore art cannot work that way."

Seated Man, *1922, bronze, 20" high.*

Woman with Book, *1919, stone, 16½" high.*

Bather III, *1917, bronze, 28½" high.*

92

Pierrot, *1925, bronze, 5" high.*

MOTHER AND CHILD

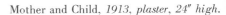

The theme of *Mother and Child,* nourished by the events and desires of his life, had engrossed Lipchitz from his earliest years as a sculptor. He made his first *Mother and Child* in 1913. Another version followed in 1914-15, shortly after his return from Spain.

In 1930 he conceived a new version. This is the story he told me about it:

"I made sketches. I knew what I wanted to do, but I didn't know the aspect of it. As I generally do, I made numerous sketches to find out. One day I was on the terrace of my house in Paris and I saw a cloud formation. I immediately related this form to my *Mother and Child.* I hurried down to my studio to capture this formation in a sketch. From there emerged the final aspect of this *Mother and Child.* It's like that with all of my sculptures. Behind every one is some kind of a story."

Here in America, shortly after his arrival in 1941, he made *Return of the Child,* his first and only work in granite in the United States. He had to abandon working in stone, a medium he used a great deal during his Paris period, because of bursitis. The drawings for this sculpture were made in France before his flight to America.

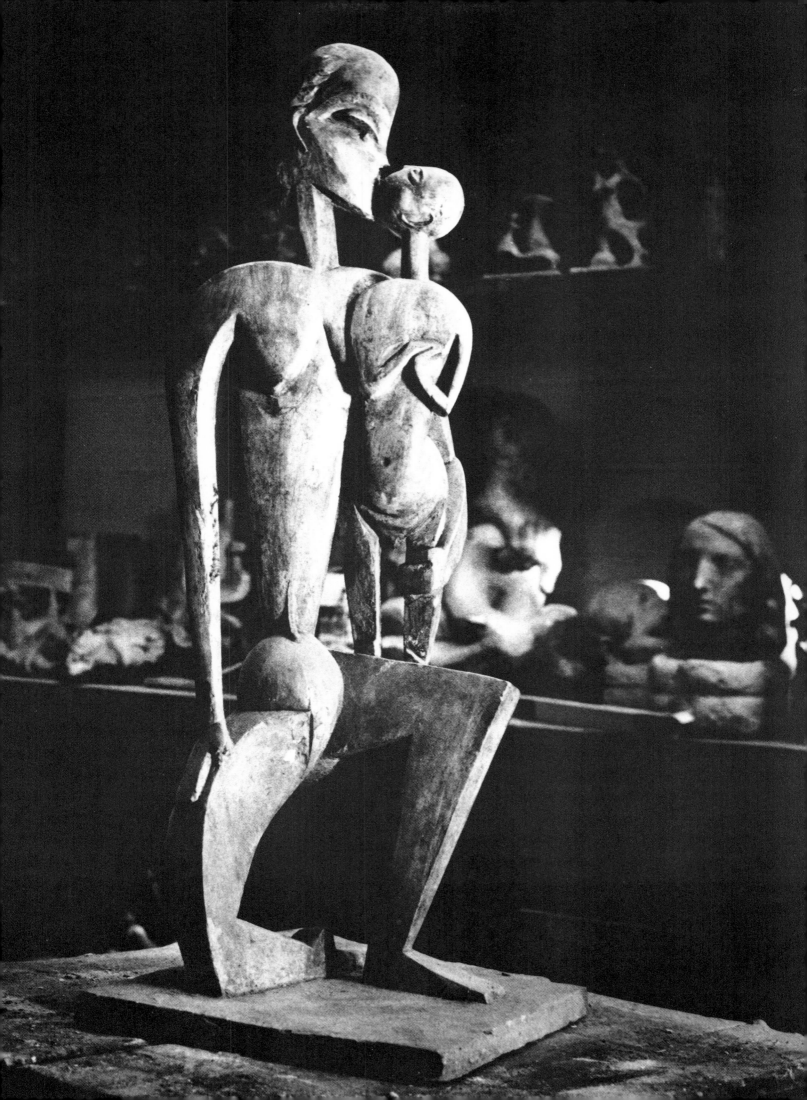

Mother and Children,
*1914-1915, bronze,
28¾" high.*

Mother and Child,
*1929-1930, bronze,
51¼" high.*

Sketch for Mother and Child *with hands, 1939.*

Lipchitz speaks of having been "pregnant" with this work for a long time; when at last he was able to start, the forms were preconceived in his mind. He tried to explain his preoccupation with this theme:

"There is always in me this desire to return to the Mother—the source of life. It is very complicated and complex to explain. I believe it has something to do with my work. As Cubists we were so far apart from nature, you know, that perhaps I have a kind of guilt complex in my subconscious mind. I always have the feeling that I have to come back to the beginning."

Filled with pain and despair a Mother without legs and hands extends her arms imploringly to the sky while her helpless child clings to her. Despite the pathos of the tragic figure, there emerges hope. This *Mother and Child,* which stands in the sculpture garden of the Museum of Modern Art in New York, took seven years to complete—from 1939 to 1945. In the earliest studies Lipchitz had not removed her hands. He did that later, as he explains, to liberate the composition from all bounds and more clearly emphasize the tragedy of the Mother in contrast to the child embracing her—symbolizing victory for triumphant life.

Sketch for Mother and Child *without hands.*

Plaster of Mother and Child II *with arms removed.*

Mother and Child II, *1941-1945, bronze, 50" high.*

He recalled a touching story concerning this *Mother and Child*:

"After I had finished my *Mother and Child,* I suddenly remembered that I had seen once a scene more or less like this. I believe it was in 1935, while I was visiting my family in Russia. One evening I went out walking; it was quite late and raining hard. I heard a tragically beautiful voice in the distance—when I went to see where it came from, I came to a railroad station and there I saw in the hazy light a beggar woman on a little wagon. She had hands but no legs, and her hair was wet and loose from the rain, and she was singing. It was really an extraordinary vision for me which probably went deep into my subconscious mind, for I did not remember it when I worked on the sculpture."

In 1948, while his wife was expecting Lolya, he conceived again a Mother and Child. The extreme pathos and violence of the earlier versions are gone. The bodies, once taut with

tension and pain, are now tranquil and serene. The mother fully holds the child in her tenderness and love.

It was this deep desire to have a child of his own that more than anything else influenced the recurring theme. The obsession of the Mother and Child motif was lodged deep in the core of his imagination. First felt as early as 1913, the birth of Lolya in 1948 fulfilled his longing and made this his final version.

"When my daughter was born we were living on Washington Square and I used to take her out in her carriage. I felt happy and inspired while I was pushing this cart. Out of this feeling I made the sculpture *Cradle*. In the composition you can see the push cart, the wheels, and the child in the heart, the center. What does the bird on top represent? I could not tell you exactly. Perhaps because I was flying with happiness, not touching the earth."

Return of the Child, *1941, bronze, 45" high.*

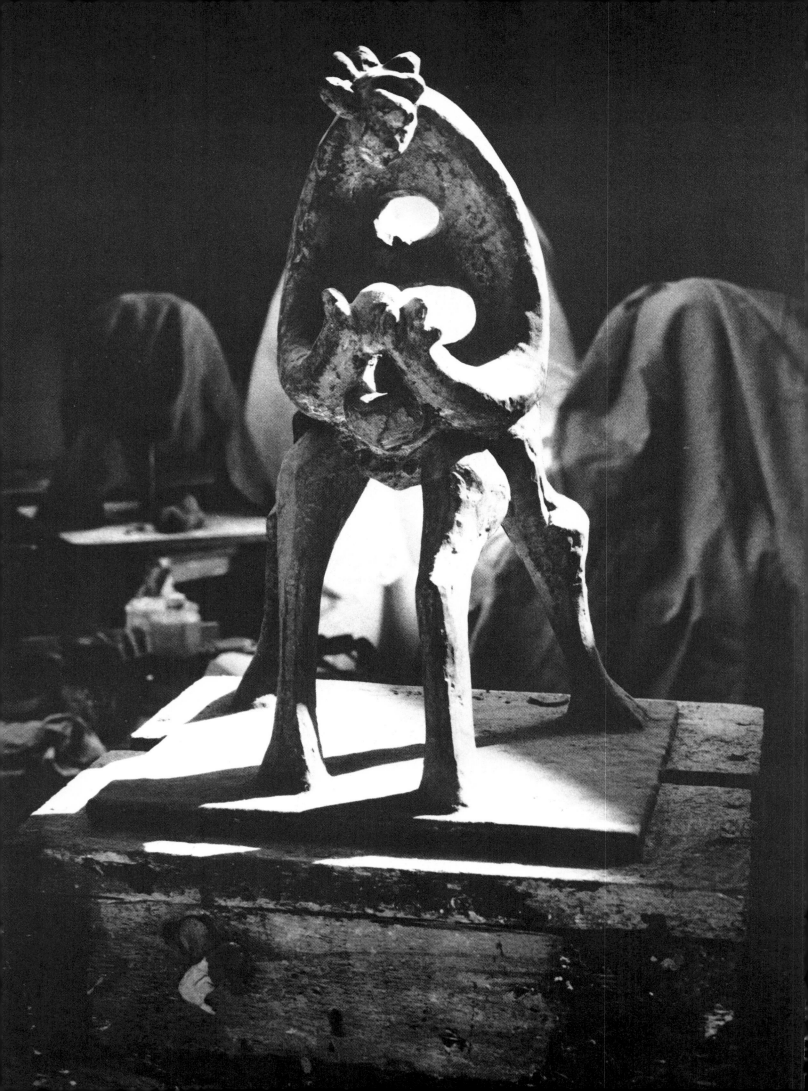

The Cradle,
1948, bronze, 32″ high.

Mother and Child, *1948, bronze, 15½″ high*.

Lipchitz applies the patina to Mother and Child, *1949.*

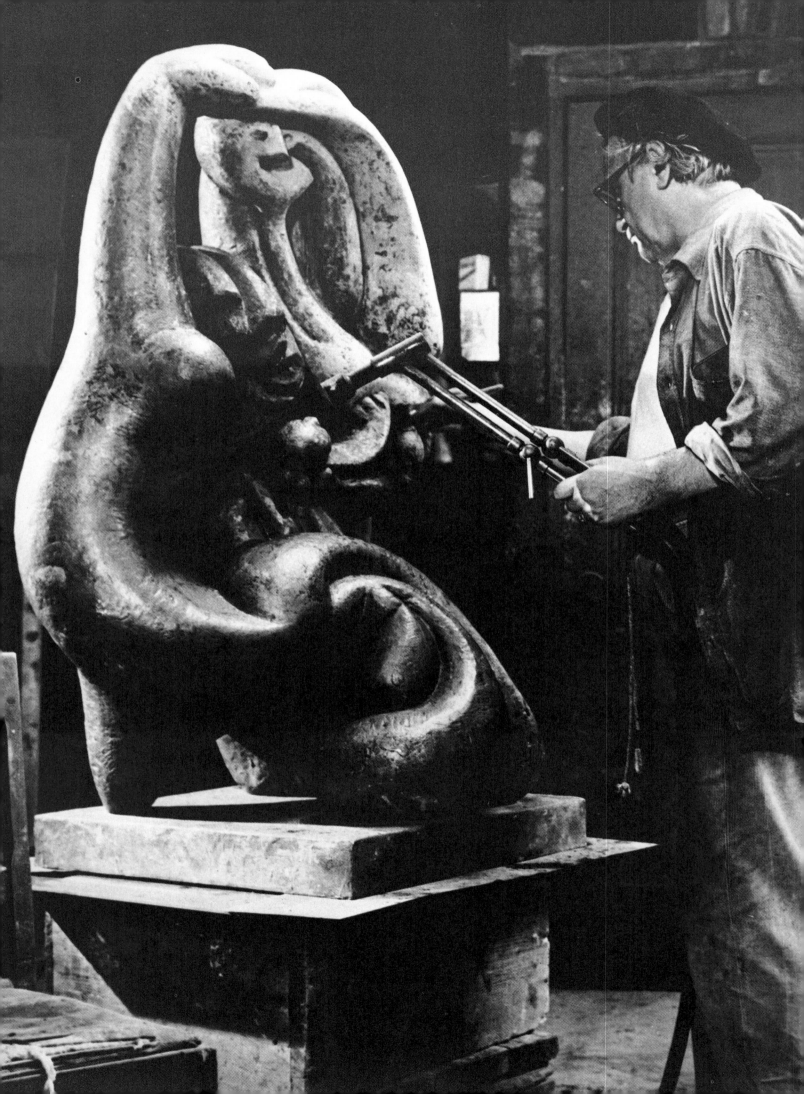

Sketch for Mother and Child, *1949.*

...her and Child, *1949, bronze, 46½″ high.*

PORTRAITS

Mother and Child, *1949-1958, bronze, 52" high.*

W hile discussing with Lipchitz his many portraits, I commented on various Cubist portraits by his colleagues Picasso, Gris, Braque. I seemed to have struck a sensitive nerve, because he became very excited and said: "I have never made an abstract portrait. I have only made abstract heads!"

When I questioned him about his distinction between portraits and abstract heads he explained: "Well, you see, my Cubist friends were all making Cubist portraits. I was always against that. I had long discussions about it, especially with my good friend Gris. I felt, and still do, that it is not

legitimate, because a portrait is something absolutely different. It has to do with likeness, with psychology, and at the same time it must be a work of art. I feel that you cannot alter it, you have to make it realistic, and I never made a Cubist portrait. All my portraits are realistic."

Once a laborer came to Lipchitz's studio in Paris to pick up a sculpture for shipment. On a sudden impulse Lipchitz pointed alternately to an abstract head and a portrait and asked the man which he would take if he had a choice. The man thought awhile, studying both subjects, and then pointed to the abstract head. Lipchitz was astonished over this choice and asked him why. The worker replied: "Because this one makes me think, while I know what the other is."

In his foundry-studio Lipchitz was retouching the wax of *Head* which he made in 1915. This is a key work because it represents a new phase in his style. The analytical Cubist elements now had saturated his imagination and had resulted in the controlled stylization of this and many other Cubist sculptures that followed.

The wax of *Head* is supported by sticks, which are especially necessary during the summer months. Once it took Lipchitz three weeks to repair an arm that had melted in a sudden heat wave.

Lipchitz begins a work with sketches (also called *maquettes*) in terra cotta or plasticine. During the war years he became accustomed to making a lot of drawings for sculptures, which he continues to do. They are mostly spontaneous visions which he then develops

to clarify the composition. His drawings already comprehend the many variations that often develop out of a theme. Instinctively he catches on paper what later will emerge in bronze.

I have seen him start either with sketches on paper or small three-dimensional sketches or *maquettes* in plasticine. He makes the *maquettes* without armature in order to remain free for changes and developments as he goes along. He concentrates on harmonious line and composition rather than details, critically studying the silhouette of his sketch. Yet when he makes a portrait he always starts with three-dimensional sketches rather than preparatory drawings.

In 1920 in Paris, Lipchitz made a portrait of Gertrude Stein. She was an ardent admirer of Picasso and a patron of the Cubists, but she did not like sculpture. Lipchitz felt that she was an exceptional subject and persuaded her to sit for him. "She looked like a Buddha then," he recalled.

During the sitting he tried, in his own words, to "brainwash her" to a liking for sculpture, but it did not work; she did not have the feeling for it. Nevertheless, they became lasting friends. In 1938 he wanted to make another portrait of her and started with sketches in terra cotta. "She had shrunk a little and looked like an old Rabbi," he said, describing her changed appearance. But then the war came and Lipchitz was not able to finish the portrait. In 1944 in America he began to make a study after the earlier sketches, but he was never quite satisfied with the likeness.

Throughout my visits with Lipchitz I had been curious about what it was like to pose for him and watch him work on a portrait. Then one day in the studio I met a well-known surgeon who was sitting for his portrait. Later he told me that the experiences from sitting to sitting were quite exciting. "One day Lipchitz made me and the next he destroyed me. This went on for weeks and for many sittings, until he finally was satisfied."

Lipchitz put it in a different way: "To make a portrait is a very intimate thing—almost like getting married. You have to study and analyze the person and dig deep into his or her hidden characteristics."

Chimène, *1930, bronze, 18″ high.*

The Japanese Basket (*à la limite du possible*),
1958, bronze, 20″ high.

Head, *1933, bronze, 9″ high.*

I knew that for several years Lipchitz had been working on a portrait of his wife Yulla. I saw a covered head that had been set aside in the studio, and when I asked him what it was he was evasive. Several days later, when I arrived at the studio in the late morning, the head was uncovered and he was working on it, with Mrs. Lipchitz sitting for him.

As if to excuse himself, he said: "I don't know if I can do a good job with her, she is too close to me. Besides, she won't come to enough sittings."

I took out my camera and started shooting. While he stepped back for a moment to study his progress, Mrs. Lipchitz slipped off her chair and curiously peered at her husband's

work. After looking at the portrait intently, she stepped back as if to give it a final view.

"Oh, she complained, "the nose is much too big."

"No, no," he said, "your nose is very beautiful. What do you want?"

Mrs. Lipchitz wasn't happy at all.

To stop her complaining, he added with a sly little smile: "If you are not quiet, I will make you a bigger nose!"

I asked him if he had ever made a self-portrait. He shook his head and said: "I guess I don't like myself that much."

Little Italian, *1911, bronze, 11″ high.*

The plaster cast of Little Italian.

ead of Mlle. S.,
911, bronze, 19¾" high.

Portrait of Mme. Jaffe, *plaster.*

Study for Portrait of Gertrude Stein, *1938, 11½″ high.*

Jean Cocteau, *1920, marble, 14″ high.*

Lipchitz applies the final touches to Portrait of Sturgis Ingersoll *before it is cast.*

Portrait of Sturgis Ingersoll, *1960, plasticine, 17½″ high.*

HANDLE WITH CARE

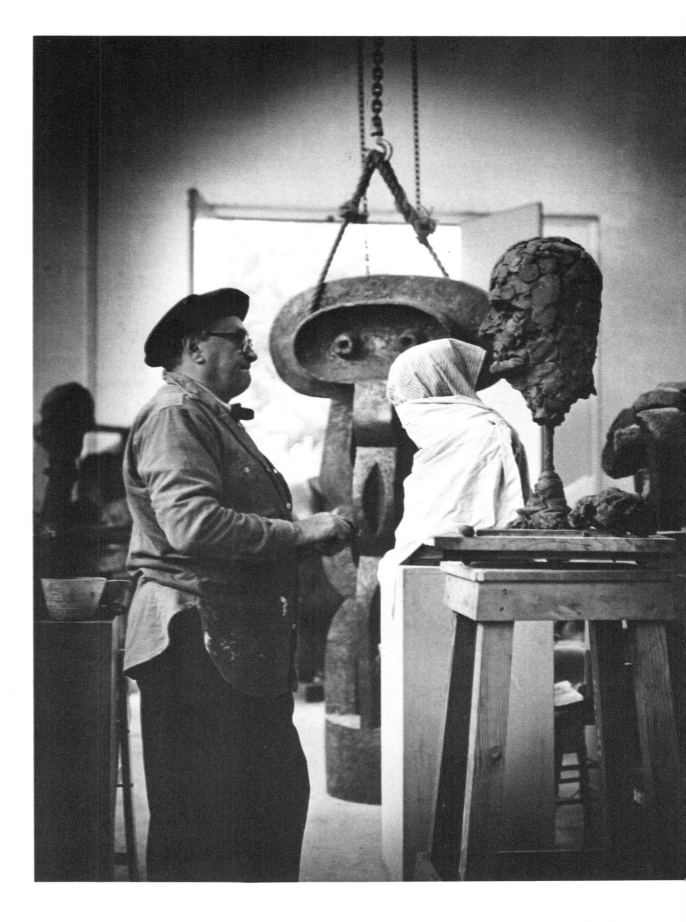

Lipchitz frequently works from memory before the initial sitting.

A view of the studio.

At right—an unfinished version of Miracle.

At left—a bronze of Prodigal Son, *1931.*

1912–1933

Woman of Woman with Gazelles, *1912, bronze, 46½″ high.*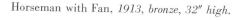

Horseman with Fan, *1913, bronze, 32″ high.*

Cubism combined conception and objectivity, an achievement which has made it a philosophy, a point of view, rather than a "school."

"We Cubists often have had a slight guilt complex because knowingly we have deviated from nature," Lipchitz explained. "For us Cubism meant liberation from conventional views and forms, freedom from naturalism. There was nothing from which to begin. We first had to destroy the old and then we had to invent our own forms and colors. It was a great challenge to our imagination and our faith."

Lipchitz has emphasized many times that he did not follow the same technical imperatives that the Cubist painters did. His struggle was quite different. Not being satisfied any longer with the existing forms and patterns, he felt the need to "blow up" the existing structures and start again at the very beginning of evolution.

139

Lipchitz did not work within the Cubist idiom until around 1915, although his painter colleagues had started much earlier. Recalling those days, he said:

"Cubism was a kind of collective work. It is difficult to differentiate exactly which belongs to one or the other. We were working together in a joint effort, exchanging our discoveries and ideas, one inspiring the other. We were like a big family.

"Once with Gris I went to see Picasso. At that time he was working on a painting which he called *Si tu Veux*. It is a harlequin who has in one hand the music to a little song called 'Si tu Veux' and under the other arm a violin. This painting was very curiously made with a lot of sand and different colors. Picasso asked Gris whether he liked it, and Gris said: 'Yes, I do, very much.' Then he asked me, and I said: 'I don't like it. It is too complicated for me.' Gris became very angry with me when we left, but I said: 'I have to tell him what I think of it when he asks me. That is what we are friends for.' What surprised me was that when I saw this painting sometime later it was completely changed, simplified. The painting is now at the Rosenberg Gallery, and when you look at it you still see how it was before. It was chaotic. You can still see the traces of the sand."

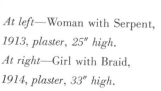

At left—Woman with Serpent,
1913, plaster, 25" high.
At right—Girl with Braid,
1914, plaster, 33" high.

Encounter, *1913, lead, 32" high.*

Sailor with Guitar, *1914, plaster, 30″ high.*

During my first days of photographing Lipchitz's sculpture in the studio and the foundry, he would watch me constantly while continuing with his work but would never ask questions or make a comment. Perhaps his admitted fear of mechanical things aroused his curiosity about the mechanics of photography. Sometimes he would walk across the camera's view field, trying to catch a glimpse of what I was preparing to do. At the end of my preparations I asked him if he would like to look through the camera to see the result, but he declined. "No, thank you, I can see that you don't need help from me."

His concern was understandable—he wanted his sculptures to be represented in their true conception. To photograph sculpture is a difficult and challenging task. Since sculpture is three-dimensional, it is dependent on the effects of light and shadow in the picture. And the sculptor, in creating a certain form, is guided and inspired by the play of light falling on his work. If the photographer does not understand the sculptor's language, he easily might misrepresent the artist's work.

Seated Guitar Player, *1918, bronze, 23⅝″ high.*

Seated Guitar Player, *1920, bronze, 20½″ high.*

Pierrot with Clarinet, *1919, plaster, 31″ high.*

Seated Man with Guitar, *1922, bronze, 15⅝″ high.*

Pierrot with Mandolin, *1925, bronze, 18½″ high.*

Musical Instruments, *1924, bronze, 19¼″ high.*

Man with Guitar, *1925, bronze, 23¼″ high.*

Seated Man, *1925, bronze, 22″ high.*

Bust of a Woman, *1932, bronze, 7½″ high*

Germaine,

The Harpists, *1930, bronze, 17" high.*

Hands, *1933, bronze, 21⅛″ high.*

From left to right—
Harlequin à la Mandoline, *1932, bronze, 26″ high.*
Baigneuse, *1917, bronze, 28½″ high.*
Harlequin à la Clarinette, *1919, bronze, 29″ high.*

At right—Figure, *1916, plaster, 49½″ high.*
Above—*plaster of* Mlle. S., *1911, 19¾″ high.*
Center—*plaster of* Encounter, *1913, 32″ high.*

Harlequin with Mandolin, *1924-1925, oval relief—bronze, 50″ high.*

Maquettes for Figure, *1926, terra-cotta, 8½″ to 10″ high.*

PLOUMANACH

Figure, *1926-1930, bronze, 84" high.*

Lipchitz was deeply absorbed in his work, retouching the wax of *Ploumanach*. It was hot in the foundry and the room was filled with the smell of burnt wax. I could see little pearls of sweat on his face as he lifted the hot iron from the gas burner and with a slight hiss touched the surface of *Ploumanach*, leaving behind a trace of smoke.

He turned to me and sighed, "Ah—I wish I could feel the cool breeze of Ploumanach right now!" I knew what he meant. The sculpture *Ploumanach* was named after a little seaside resort in Brittany where Lipchitz had spent a summer vacation. Not far from the historic stone alignments of Carnac, which have been traced back to the Neolithic Age, Ploumanach's coast line is an extraordinary sight. Huge rocks, often piled on others, leap up from the wild currents of the North Atlantic. The bases of the rocks are washed out and shaky, causing the piled-up stones to sway in stormy weather.

For many reasons Lipchitz could never part with the original sculpture of Ploumanach, which was made of ebony. Just recently his younger brother Rubin, who takes care of the studio in Boulonge-sur-Seine, had shipped it to America where it was put in his Hastings-on-Hudson studio.

Having completed the wax, Lipchitz was now ready to have *Ploumanach* cast in bronze. He put his tools away and turned to me. "Are you finished?" he asked. This was the sign that he wanted to take a break and relax. We stepped out the door of the foundry into the cool air, stretching and enjoying the pause. But my curiosity was never stilled, and he knew it.

"*Ploumanach* is the only sculpture you made in wood, isn't it?"

"Yes, that is true. I always wanted to make a wood sculpture, and decided to make Ploumanach out of ebony. But is it not very durable; the wood cracks and I have to repair

160

it from time to time—that's why I never wanted to sell it. I made the sculpture with a shaky bottom in the form of an arch, because the stones are like that. But the weight of the top part is too heavy for the arch, so I later made the sculpture in bronze and now I have added the base."

"*Ploumanach* already has freer forms. When exactly did you abandon Cubism?"

"I am still a Cubist, and as long as I am guided by the elements of my imagination I will be a Cubist. If you ask how I came to make freer forms, I can only say—this is a matter of growth and development. It is just as if you had asked me how I became an adult from a child."

He sat down and motioned me to join him.

"You know, that reminds me of an episode a few years ago when a young couple came to my studio to buy a sculpture. The young woman was very beautiful. She looked around for a long while and then picked *Encounter*. We came to an agreement, and as they were about to leave she asked: 'Mr. Lipchitz, tell me, did I make a good choice?' I said: 'Madam, I cannot tell you. My children are all the same to me.' But she insisted: 'Oh, Mr. Lipchitz, you know!' Her smile weakened me somewhat and I said: 'Look, you chose a sculpture that I made in 1913. Don't you think I've made some progress since then?' You see, she wanted me to tell her: 'Yes, Madam, you made a good choice, and so on.' But I am not a salesman. Even though I needed the money badly, I didn't make the sale."

After a thoughtful pause he added: "You know, everybody looks, but very few people see—because in order to see you have to think."

"Do you feel that coming to America influenced your work at all?" I continued.

"No," he replied, "I don't believe it had any influence on my work. When I came I was fifty years old; I was a formed man and I could not be influenced any longer. But as a person it gave me new life and vigor. I felt rejuvenated. Despite all the terrible things that had happened to me in the war, I felt really marvelous when I came; I was like a newborn child. You know, at first I did not want to come to America because I feared that I would find only concrete and steel here. But, of course, I was wrong. Immediately I liked this country very much."

"I can imagine that the skyline of New York overwhelmed you when you saw it for the first time?"

"Oh, yes! The skyscrapers made a tremendous impression on me. When I came into New York Harbor for the first time, the skyline was an extraordinary sight, the like of which I had never seen before. Many times I went to Staten Island just to experience that feeling again, but it was never quite the same."

With care the wax is poured into the mold.

The sculptor applies the finishing touches to the wax model.

A mold is made from the wax model
and the metal then is poured for casting.

165

Finally, the patina is applied to Ploumanach, *1926, 31″ high.*

PROMETHEUS

Two themes have been ever-recurring through Lipchitz's life. One is Mother and Child, the other Prometheus. Twice his attempts to create an enduring Prometheus were thwarted—first, in Paris in 1938, where his gigantic *Prometheus Strangling the Vulture* was attacked and torn down as being subversive; then, several years later, in Rio de Janeiro.

In 1943 he received a commission to make a monumental work for the Ministry of Health and Education in Rio de Janeiro, and he chose again the theme of Prometheus. The Ministry's funds were low, so Lipchitz suggested that he make a small model, one-third the original size, send this to Brazil, and have it enlarged and cast in bronze there. Then he would come to Brazil and put the finishing touches on it.

All agreed that this was a fine solution, and Lipchitz poured all his powers into the sculpture. When the model was completed, it was sent to Brazil and Lipchitz awaited its enlargement.

Lipchitz explains the unfortunate experience that followed:

"One day, maybe a year later, I received a phone call from *Time Magazine;* a journalist wanted to speak to me about the placing of my bronze sculpture on the wall of the Ministry of Education and Health building. I explained to her that this was impossible; it would take at least another year, because it had to be enlarged. 'But,' she said, 'we received a story from our correspondent. Let me come to your studio, please, and we can talk about it.'

"I showed her all the papers, all my contracts, and she went away convinced that the correspondent's report had been wrong.

tch for Prometheus Strangling the Vulture, *1936, bronze.*

"A week later she called me again and said: 'Mr. Lipchitz, I received a roll of film this morning with pictures of your statue. Your bronze statue was placed on the wall.'

"I was worried and I said: 'Could I come to see you so that you would show me the pictures?' I went. She showed me the photographs, and I saw a real catastrophe! My little model of seven feet was cast, badly cast, and placed on this enormous wall. It looks like a pin on it. I was sick about it and angry, and I asked my friends what to do. But nobody could help me. The only thing I can say now is that it is not my sculpture. When people look at it, they can only think that the sculptor had no sense of proportion to make such a little thing for that big wall. But I am not responsible, and I say that it is not my sculpture!"

The plaster cast for Lipchitz's 1943 *Prometheus* remained in his studio on Washington Square. But miraculously it did not perish in the flames of 1952, because a few weeks before the fire Joseph Fraser, Director of the Pennsylvania Academy of Fine Arts, had selected it for an annual exhibition. Despite Lipchitz's reservations about letting him have

Model for Prometheus Strangling the Vulture, *1936, bronze.*

it because the plaster was too large and extremely difficult to transport, Mr. Fraser persisted, and the sculpture was put on exhibition in Philadelphia the week before his studio burned out. On January 4, 1952, one day before the fire, Lipchitz received in Philadelphia the George Widener Gold Metal for his *Prometheus*.

Since Philadelphia in fact had saved this sculpture, the Academy of Fine Arts commissioned Lipchitz to have it cast in bronze for them. The only other existing cast is owned by the Walker Art Center in Minneapolis.

Lipchitz explained to me his own personal interpretation of the mythical figure of Prometheus: "When I was asked to do a sculpture for the Palace of Science at the 1937 World's Fair in Paris, I pondered what to make. I said to myself: 'Science is progress and progress is related in our conscious mind with Prometheus. He brought us light and fire, he brought us medicine, he taught us a lot of things. But in the Greek myth, Prometheus was enchained and the vulture was eating his liver. If he were still enchained, there would be no progress.' Therefore, I took away his chains and had him strangle the vulture."

Prometheus Strangling the Vulture II, *1944-1953, plaster, 8½' high*

170

PROMETHEUS STRANGLING THE VULTURE 1944
by JACQUES LIPCHITZ, 1891–
Purchased
Lisa Norris Elkins Fund

MIRACLE

Prometheus Strangling the Vulture II, *1944-1953, bronze, Philadelphia Museum of Fine Arts, 8½' high.*

Miracle II,
1947, bronze,
30¾″ high.

My sculpture is always related to my life," Lipchitz told me. "As soon as I acquired the knowledge of my language, I started to tell stories through my work, and these stories come from my everyday life, my actions, dreams, and hopes."

After the war, Jewish refugees throughout Europe, North Africa, and the Middle East were waiting to go to Israel. With the lifting of the immigration ban, they streamed in by the thousands, and with them went the heart of Lipchitz. For Lipchitz, too, the creation of a Jewish homeland was hope about to be fulfilled. As his prayer of thanksgiving he created *Miracle II*. The outer fringes of the Tablets of Moses burst into the flames of a candelabrum, and before it stands a figure, arms raised to the Tablets, exalted in hope and prayer.

Looking through the window of Lipchitz's studio and seeing scores of silent, unmoving figures standing around, one might get the impression that this big building has no human occupant. Sometimes, when I entered the studio, I would think I was alone until I found Lipchitz quietly absorbed behind one of his statues. By now I was familiar with most of his sculptures. He had told me many stories about them and of the problems and joys he had experienced in creating them.

The work of a sculptor is a very time-consuming process. Sometimes Lipchitz moves about slowly, observing, weighing, thinking; other times his movements are quick and short, as if he is hurrying to catch an image that has just come to him. Once in awhile he makes grunting sounds of approval or disapproval. It is far less spectacular than seeing him work in the foundry where the fire, the melting of the metals, and the colorful sparks from the meeting of chemicals with fire set an exciting scene.

He is not a carver, but a modeler. The difference is that the carver starts with a big block of material and carves it down to the desired shape and size, while the modeler starts with a small chunk of material and adds to it until the object of his imagination emerges, often many times the size he started with. Sometimes, however, Lipchitz takes a long bush knife or even a common kitchen knife and carves out the shape he wants. His most important tools, of course, are his hands, his right thumb playing the leading role.

His concept of a work is in a constant state of organic flux; he never stops making changes until he has achieved perfection. And of each new idea he makes sketches. He relies a great deal on the immediacy of the sketching technique to pull the image out of the flux of his imagination. Before a work emerges in bronze he may have done countless sketches.

Following the initial sketch is usually a model, three times smaller than the final cast, made of wax or pliable plasticine. He makes an armature out of sticks and pieces of wire to support the model. Large armatures, however, are made for him. For the actual modeling he prefers to work with plasticene, which is nonhardening. He applies it in large lumps pressed into place and carved out with a kitchen knife or his large bush knife. For the succeeding step, the plaster cast, he hires a professional caster. As soon as the plaster cast has hardened, he again goes to work on it, filing, changing, adding, repairing. The work is still in evolution, and with chisel and file he continues to perfect his composition. After the plaster cast, a wax model is prepared, which is the last step before the bronze casting. The wax is prepared at the foundry, and Lipchitz continues to work on it at his studio there with hot tools and soft beeswax, again making slight changes or correcting imperfections that occurred during the wax casting process.

The sculptor at work on a larger version of Miracle.

1938–1957

Rape of Europe, *1938, bronze, 23⅛″ high.*

Arrival, *1941, bronze, 21″ high.*

Pilgrim,
1942, bronze,
31½" high.

Theseus, *1942, plaster, 25¼″ high.*

Joy of Orpheus, *1945, bronze, 20½″ high.*

Song of Songs, *1945-1948, bronze, 23½" x 36".*

Hagar II, *1949, bronze, 13¼″ high.*

Rescue II, *1947, bronze, 19″ high.*

Study for Sacrifice, *1948-1949, bronze, 19½" high.*

SONG OF THE VOWELS

Sacrifice III, *1949-1957, bronze, 49¼″ high.*

Song of the Vowels, *1931-1953, bronze, 10' high.*

Lipchitz was standing on top of his huge totem *Song of the Vowels*. With tremendous force he hammered in a section of the sculpture, and I recalled something he had said earlier. When asked by a visitor at the foundry if this work was not too strenuous for him, he replied: "When I don't work I feel sick. When I work I get very tired. But I'd rather be tired than sick."

Jacques Lipchitz is a deeply religious man. He was brought up in the orthodox faith, yet he could not accept orthodoxy because it denies representation. "After all," he said, "representation is one of the key elements in a work of art. For over fifty years I have been a sculptor and many times I have asked myself—what is this force that drives me continually to make sculpture? Well, you know, art is religion. I don't know how the two can be separated. For me sculpture is divinity. This is the only answer that I could find for myself. Art is man's distinctly human way of fighting death. Through art, man achieves immortality and in this immortality we find God."

He has interpreted many religious themes in his life through sculptures. *Song of the Vowels* is one. Inspired by a prayer sung by the priests and priestesses of ancient Egypt—a jubilant chorus of vowels that lend themselves to the uninterrupted flow of melody—he conceived this harp-shaped sculpture. It evolved from a smaller work called *Harpists* which he made in 1930. *Song of the Vowels* was completed in 1931 and purchased by Mme. de Mandrot for her villa in Le Pradet in France. After her death it was moved to the Kunsthaus in Zurich, Switzerland. A second cast belongs to the Rockefeller Collection.

Song of the Vowels is a transparency sculpture, saturated with light and air. Having exploited the geometrical Cubist concept to its fullest, he attempted in his transparencies

to free the mass of his sculptures from its traditional boundaries. One quiet evening at home Lipchitz explained to me how he came to make his first transparency:

"Since my beginning as a sculptor I have been searching for ways to make sculpture as rapidly as my imagination worked, so that my hands could follow my imagination. The revelation didn't come to me until one evening when I attended a lecture on art at the Sorbonne. The guest speaker had such a heavy foreign accent that I could not follow him, so I became completely absorbed in myself. Suddenly, in a flash, I realized how to make sculpture that would be transparent. I rushed back to my studio and built from cardboard a little sculpture *(Pierrot, 1925)*. The next morning I went to the foundry with it. Valsuani's brother-in-law, Monsieur Spohr, was doing my work then, and when he saw the model he said, 'You are crazy; this cannot be cast.' But I said, 'Let's try.' I made it in wax right there and we started to calculate where to put the gates and so on. A few days later it was cast. Except for a few small flaws, it came out well. This gave me courage. For over five years I was obsessed with these transparencies; they had a tremendous influence on me and on sculpture in general. All the welding techniques used in sculpture today came afterward and were adopted from my transparencies. For years I had an absolute feeling of discovery. But when I started to cool off and looked around me, I saw that it had existed before, even in ancient Egyptian sculpture. And I learned an important lesson—that it is not the technique that is important, but what one does with it. There are no new techniques under the sun. The only thing that is new is the feeling, the impression the artist wants to convey."

OUR TREE OF LIFE

Lesson of a Disaster, *1952-1962, plaster, 12' high.*

Returning from the foundry in the late afternoon, Lipchitz wanted to stop at the studio to show me something. I asked him what it was but he would not tell me. "Wait, I'll show you," he replied.

Opening the door, he walked straight over to a large plasticene sculpture, picked up his knife, and proceeded to work on it without an explanation or comment. After awhile he looked at me and said: "You see when I agreed to make a Virgin for the Catholic church, I promised myself I would make something that represented the essence of my own Jewish religion as soon as I had completed the Virgin. I have been brooding about it for a long time, and now it is coming to me. I am working on it. I want it to show the dynamic powers of my religion. I call it: *Our Tree of Life* — our Jewish Tree of Life."

The studio was beginning to darken as twilight approached. The light was no longer right for Lipchitz to work. He put his tools down and motioned me to follow him to one corner of the room, where we sat down, relaxing. For a long time neither of us spoke. I

had been associated with Lipchitz for more than three years. I had been with him from morning till late at night, sometimes for many weeks, and we had grown quite close during this time. My gaze wandered back and forth across his huge studio, across an astonishing portion of work, much of which I had photographed. But there were still many things I had not asked him—questions that were hard to ask and even more difficult to answer.

"Jacques," I said, "What would you say left the greatest impact on you and your work?"

"Generations who lived before me, in the old times and in modern times, are around me and have influenced me."

"But what about those artists who claim that their way is completely their own? Is your way not your own?"

"I did not fall from the sky, and neither did anybody else fall from the sky. If anybody tells you that they did, you had better be very suspicious!"

The artist at work on Our Tree of Life.

Interior of studio.
At left, Between Heaven and Earth.
At right, Lesson of a Disaster.

Our Tree of Life, *plasticine*.

"What about the influence of Cubism? You often hear that Cubism was for the Cubists a formula, by which . . ."

"No, no, no," he interrupted, "not at all. Cubism is not a formula, it is not a school. Cubism is a philosophy, a point of view in the universe. It is like standing at a certain point on a mountain and looking around. If you go higher, things will look different; if you go lower, again they will look different. It is a point of view."

On a shelf nearby I noticed a piece of African carving and was reminded of another claim that art historians make — the influence of African art on Cubism. But Lipchitz explained the relationship between African art and Cubism in a much different way.

"Our generation had come to a crossroad," he said. "We could take the way of traditional, representative art, or we could take the way of the imagination. We took the latter, of course, and along this road we came across many other civilizations which had also taken the road of their imagination. The African Negro and the Mexican Indian, among others."

I persisted: "Don't you think that African Negro art has had any direct influence on Cubism?"

"Very little," he said, "very little. Our art is almost entirely of western civilization and doesn't have much to do with the others."

"Jacques, you mentioned once that you made drawings that were almost blueprints for your early Cubist sculptures. Was this not something of a formula?"

"Oh, yes, but I did that only for a short time. I soon learned that it did not help me very much."

"I imagine that this was too confining?"

"Yes, because the final judge is the eye. I learned to trust my eyes. You know, it is the same thing when you photograph me. The beginner uses a formula, but soon he

learns to trust his eyes. You trust your eyes more than the dials on your camera, no? If you had looked only at the dials on the camera, I would not have allowed you to continue to photograph me!"

He went on: "When I learned to trust my eyes, I became a little freer. Freedom has to be taken, it is not given. You have to fight for it, you understand. This was my way of fighting for freedom."

It was getting dark in the studio. Lipchitz, a bit restless, got up and started walking around. I packed up my gear and together we went outside. He mentioned a visit which we had made some weeks ago to the Guggenheim Museum. I asked him why he was so much against nonobjective art.

"I am a potential enemy of this art, if you can call it art, because I feel that this art is mostly a dead end, far apart from life, apart from what a work of art should be. Maybe

it is just decorative art. But it does not communicate with me. I don't find any door for its entrance."

Driving back to his house, we were quietly lost in our thoughts. I was thinking over the years of my association with Lipchitz and I felt a little sad, now that my job was almost finished. In all the time we had been together, there was one question I had never asked. It was the most difficult question to ask an artist. When I finally did, that evening in the car, he smiled at first, as if to say, I was wondering when you would ask me that.

"All my life as an artist I have asked myself: What pushes me continually to make sculpture? I have found the answer—at least the answer for myself. Art is an action against death. It is denial of death. All living things have their way to fight death. The animals have procreation. But art is man's unique way of fighting death and achieving immortality. And in this continuity of art, of creation and denial of death, we find God."

LIPCHITZ

an evaluation by Alfred Werner

We are concerned here with an authentic sculptor,
something extremely rare. The importance of an artist can only be
measured by the intensity of the desire which his work itself
expresses to escape from the tyranny of the formula in order to
find beneath it the true tradition. I invite you to the noble spectacle
of the struggle taking place between the most chaotic spiritual atmosphere
ever known, ceaselessly changing forms, and a free intelligence
endeavoring to stabilize the universe.

ELIE FAURE

The function of art has been described as man's search to express the invisible by means of the visible. Anyone dealing with Jacques Lipchitz' art will find it difficult to surpass this definition as a summation of the sculptor's lifelong endeavor to link the inner world with the outer, to plumb the unfathomable sphere beneath the surface of reality, to reveal by way of the senses the wellsprings of the soul. In him we have an artist eager to communicate what he knows to those who do not yet know, an artist for whom a sculpture is the appropriate form in which to embody an innermost feeling or thought, an artist who tries to create lasting symbols of what is essential and timeless rather than to capture the mutable aspect of things. In him we have a modeler whose hands knead such inert material as plasticine or clay into the shapes of eternal life, an artist who belongs to no age. He is at once modern and primeval, wedding the abstract to the human. His quest for ordered simplification eliminates the merely incidental.

Lipchitz' art is the very antithesis of that naturalism which aims at achieving a complete resemblance to an object or scene. The imitation of nature has never been art's principal aim, and the most sterile periods in the history of art have been those in which the leading artists spent their energies trying to make the most faithful replicas of man and the world around him. It is, of course, necessary that the artist be able to re-create the images offered to his eyes, for he needs the shapes of everyday life as mnemonic aids, as raw material eventually to be transformed into meaningful symbols. Uccello was delighted to find the way to produce on a flat surface the illusion of three dimensions. But he and the artists who followed him sought far more than to place seemingly solid objects into boundless space. Perspective and all the other developments of technique were to serve the expression of inner drives, as demonstrated in the work of El Greco, who acquired all the technical refinement to be found in Cinquecento Italy and thereafter developed in Spain a vision and vitality far above the academic and orthodox.

Lipchitz, too, learned all that his predecessors could teach. An early work like the smooth, perfectly balanced *Woman with Gazelles* (1912) could not have come into being without the lessons he learned in the sculpture galleries of the Louvre. Every artist must recapitulate the stages through which successive generations of artistic forbears have passed. By the same token, every artist must free himself from the fetters of tradition to arrive at his own idiom expressive of his generation's fears and hopes. Lipchitz did this after having not only seen the El Grecos in the Prado, but also the work of fellow artists in Montparnasse, painters slightly older than himself who had already started to find new aesthetic signs and symbols.

He was fortunate enough to arrive in Paris in 1909, a period comparable in artistic importance to the early Quattrocento in Florence. Cubism, the mighty force that "destroyed" whatever remnants of the "real" world were still current, had emerged a few years earlier, and Lipchitz gradually adapted this new manifestation to his own sculptural needs. He came to agree with the writer, Guillaume Apollinaire, who, at a point when formlessness was rampant, hailed geometry as being to the artist what grammar is to the writer. The Cubist painter Albert Gleizes maintained that, in an age of surface worship, art could become real only through the operation of thought. "Cubism," Lipchitz reminisced in 1945, "was not a school, an aesthetic, or merely a discipline; it was a new view of the Universe . . . Cubism was essentially a search for a new syntax. Once this was arrived at, there was no reason for not employing it in the expression of a full message." He added, significantly: "This is what I feel I have done and what I am still trying to do. This is why I say I am still a Cubist, but expressing myself freely with all the means at my disposal from the Cubist point of view, not merely limiting myself to Cubism's syntax."

Terms like Impressionism, Fauvism, and Cubism were originated by critics whose attention had been caught by certain superficial aspects in the works of these different schools. To understand Lipchitz' statement one should bear in mind that the polyhedral volumes into which he seems to have translated the curved or angled planes found in the paintings of Picasso and Braque is the least significant feature of his work. Cubism taught mankind far more than a device to reduce forms to their fundamental shapes. The important thing it showed the artist was a road to freedom, the freedom to exaggerate, abbreviate, elongate, distort with only a minimum of reference to things observed.

In 1908, when Lipchitz was still a rather dissatisfied and frustrated student at the school of commerce in Bialystok, a "Cubist" sculpture, thousands of years old, the so-called Venus of Willendorf, was dug up in Austria. This small paleolithic limestone carving, probably a fertility symbol, is sculpturally as sound and plastically as alive as, for instance, Lipchitz' *Prometheus Strangling the Vulture*. Both the unknown artist who lived in the Aurignacian period and our contemporary Lipchitz produced works of art from skillful combinations of stereometric forms; both men were less interested in "beauty" than in vitality, less in replicas of nature than in the creation of valid symbols.

Between the *Venus* and Lipchitz' recent monumental work, the gigantic *Spirit of Enterprise*, millions of sculptures have been formed by knowing and industrious hands. Of these, only a few — those created for magical purposes — have retained their power to move the souls of men and are valid enough to communicate their magic. Although we know nothing about the Aurignacian artist, it is safe to assume that when he carved his little idol he exaggerated the female characteristics in order to stress the idea of fertility. "Magicians" on an infinitely higher level, the sculptors of the cathedral in Chartres, suggest the universe of medieval thought, above and beyond representation of human bodies. Great sculpture — from Phidias to Donatello, Michelangelo, Rodin — has always been "visible speech," to apply Dante's magnificent definition, sentences formed to utter anguish, defiance, or hope.

Changes in style are important insofar as they mirror transformations in a society or in an individual. But they are dwarfed by the common denominator, by the common desire to use art as a form of redemptive prayer. As Lipchitz once modestly put it, he wants sculpture to give us "the illusion that we are not altogether abject animals" and "the hope of some day becoming men."

Differences in media are even less important. As a young man, Lipchitz' friend Amedeo Modigliani scorned all who used "mud," Modigliani's contemptuous word for clay. Modigliani, proponent of *taille directe*, always cut right into the stone or wood, working his way inward to the image hidden, as it were, within the block. He considered himself vastly superior to the modeler who works in a soft material, building up his structure from a central core to which he adds bit by bit and subsequently casts the completed structure in bronze or some other metal. But is the use of a chisel to chip a block down to its predetermined form more "direct" than urging wax or clay into shape with one's thumb? And are not attenuated forms or thin projecting elements better suited to, say, terracotta or bronze than to carved wood or stone? There is no superiority in media, just as painting has no superiority over sculpture (a theme which engaged Leonardo da Vinci and Michelangelo in bitter polemics).

Between 1915 and 1925, that is to say, during his pre-eminently "Cubist" period, Lipchitz frequently worked in stone, although these stone sculptures were cut after clay models. Direct carving was too slow a process for his imaginative force, and he was finally to abandon carving. Yet *Man With a Guitar*, a Cubist stone figure of 1916, is no more and no less Lipchitz than the bronze *Hagar* of 1948. The sharp edges, flat planes, and solid mass of the early work is as much "Lipchitz" as is the hollowed-out lattice-work of bronze strips he did in his middle period, or the massive "baroque" forms-in-motion for which he is, perhaps, chiefly known in America. Whether firmly on the ground or almost floating in space, whether a solid block (like the lead *Figure* of 1916, which is one of his most abstract works) or a "dematerialized" transparency, a Lipchitz is always a confrontation of the artist's awestruck soul with the simultaneous crystallization of formal and emotional ideas.

Lipchitz would never claim that he was the only one who, in the revolutionary decade of 1910-20, truly understood the meaning of sculpture as a vehicle of metaphors. But he is proud of the fact that he was one of the several pathfinders who put the visible world under strict intellectual control, and who, using invention as a cudgel, knocked at the door of Truth.

From the vantage point of 1966, it may not be difficult to approve all this. Yet in 1930 an American collector, bringing *The Harpists* from France, had to resort to sophistry to appease the United States customs officials who were unwilling to classify the piece as a work of art. Since it did not have any obvious resemblance to known phenomena, it was not art and was to them an ordinary piece of dutiable metal. The owner finally convinced the customs officers that the bronze represented a legendary bird! Two years earlier progressive art had won a minor victory in the United States with Brancusi's celebrated *Bird in Flight*, when an American court reluctantly conceded that the dictionary was somewhat obsolete in its definition of sculpture's task as the imitation of natural objects. They decided that a new school of art had arisen "whose exponents attempt to portray abstract ideas."

There are only abstract ideas, and everything that deserves to be called art is in some sense abstract. Lipchitz, at an early stage in his career, came very close to pure abstraction, so close that his shapes had little resemblance to natural objects. But he felt that he could not go further in this direction, that he needed something concrete, and that by avoiding the image of man he would impoverish himself. Surveying the past fifty years of his career, one can say that nine out of ten of his sculptures resort to some embodiment of man — new, yet always recognizable. Though his work contains still lifes and compositions based on musical instruments, most of it celebrates man — bathers, sailors, harlequins, guitar players, acrobats, mothers carrying children, as well as biblical or mythological figures engaged in fateful battles. Separated by a gulf of feeling from those more attracted by inorganic forms, Lipchitz, with Goethe, believes that the aim of sculpture is "to render the dignity of man within the compass of the human form."

In order to raise questions concerning man, Lipchitz needed the image of man. But unlike the anguished Gauguin he does not merely ask: "Whence come we? What are we? Whither go we?" He knows the dread, but also its palliative. However varied his characters, the mother-child theme has been a dominant one throughout his career. At the risk of oversimplifying his philosophy, one is tempted to find in his work two major primary images to which he has clung—the mother and the beast. They alternate in his work, the beast who destroys and the female who gives birth, provides warmth, shelter, food. His themes are based on strong yet primitive urges, such as hunger and thirst, fear of death, yearning for life.

To embody these urges he has drawn upon the entire reservoir of plastic possibilities, examining the problems of balance, volume, space, hollow, and protuberance. He sought a path to metaphysical truth rather than the decorative charm which is the modest aim of so much contemporary art. His is an art of an era of crisis or, as W. H. Auden called our time, the Age of Anxiety. Those who have referred — sometimes with a malicious undertone — to the baroque character of Lipchitz' art do indeed have a point. Like the seventeenth century, ours is one of strife, disorder, schism. Lipchitz' problems are not identical with those Bernini might have found in his time. Nevertheless there is an affinity between the work of these two sculptors. Their work extends, thrusts, and spreads into space without noticeable concern for verisimilitude. Limbs are elongated, thickened or thinned out, cavities are substituted for volume, with the intention of accentuating the essential at the expense of the ephemeral. A twentieth-century Bernini, Lipchitz twists and distorts, because this is exactly what fate does to our faces and bodies, robbing them of the harmony and serenity associated with classic Greece, but compensating us for the loss of youthful charm by making us the indisputable witnesses to our own suffering. Heinrich Heine comes to mind, a chastened and chastized Jew, who no longer resents Moses for his alleged hostility to the plastic arts, since Moses himself was a great artist who "built human pyramids and carved human obelisks," — a Heine who no longer admired the Greeks who, after all, were only beautiful youths — a Heine who instead paid tribute to the Jews who "were always men, mighty, unyielding men, not only in the past, but to this very day, in spite of eighteen centuries of persecution and misery."

If, like the young Jew Heine, the young Jew Lipchitz produced what might be considered "escapist" art, with the onset of maturity he started making sculptures more in response to man's urgent needs — not carriers of social protest (which often become mere "period pieces" after the passage of a few years), but timeless, deathless metaphors, made at the point where perdition and salvation meet. In the most successful pieces, rhetoric is absent; the artist knows how to suppress unessential detail, to signify without describing, and to grasp form in movement, movement extending beyond the substance, as the light flickers from plane to plane like intricate shadows being cast upon a wall. Dreaming, praying, reflecting, brooding, his bronzes and stones are the very antithesis of the cold, immobile "classic" figure that was held up at the Ecole des Beaux-Arts as the unchallengeable ideal. Is it likely that one can walk through a hall filled with Lipchitz' work without being struck by the puzzlement, bitterness, and even terror unmasked there, without responding to the counteracting faith in life and belief in a supernatural power?

Yet these are not tracts but balanced, touchable, three-dimensional forms, sometimes overambiguous, sometimes slightly incoherent. For just as his sculptures are monumental (even those that are small are conceived in grand scale), so the problems that absorb him have possessed mankind all through time. Lipchitz cannot tell us all, for there are limits to speech, to eye and hand. Often he expects help from the astute observer who can fill in what is missing. But equally often the goal is not reached, the sound is not heard, and another heroic effort must be made by the artist who, like Prometheus, is unwilling to give up until the fire of life has become the possession of all men.

Lipchitz' statues mean nothing but themselves.
They are accessible only to those who show themselves
capable of disassociating the plastic from the
representative element, those who appreciate a
work of art exclusively for artistic reasons.

Unsigned article in B R O O M, June 1922

When the eighteen-year-old Lipchitz arrived in Paris, several paths were open to him. He might have followed in the footsteps of the deified Rodin, or by creating fashionable neoclassic figures he might have found a quick way to recognition and financial success. He might have joined the small group of rebels who had been nicknamed and now proudly called themselves Cubists. Luckily for him, he chose none of these paths, but struggled on independently, studied intensely, and looked around him with sharp eyes; he preferred to examine his own possibilities and probe his own depths rather than accept ready-made solutions.

Rodin admired a portrait bust Lipchitz had sent to the Société Nationale, but the young immigrant did not seek an introduction to the master, as anyone else would have done. Possibly the old man's expressionism was too bizarre for the neophyte who was still dedicated to pure Greek ideals. Possibly his feelings were like Brancusi's; when offered a chance to work as an assistant at Rodin's atelier, Brancusi refused, saying, "Nothing can grow under big trees." Even had Rodin's work not been alien to his own concepts, Lipchitz would have guarded his freedom above anything else. He knew very well what Picasso, Archipenko, and Boccioni were doing. He was also aware that what these men produced was decried in the Council of Paris as a "return to primitive barbarism," while docile Beaux-Arts graduates were receiving more commissions than they could execute.

He did not crave quick and ephemeral success, and preferred to develop his art from within, step by step, with the logic of necessity. Looking back at the height of his career, he remarked that there had never been abrupt changes in his work and that each new sculpture grew out of the preceding one. This is true of his pre-Cubist phase, 1911-14. Slowly he moved from academic heads and group compositions to studies in which he emphasized geometric problems and worked out principles that forecast his subsequent endorsement of Cubist aesthetics.

To appreciate, or rather to love — a word more in keeping with Lipchitz' philosophy of life — the works he did between 1914 and 1926, one need not be familiar with the history of the Cubist movement. One requires only eyes open to the beauty of lines and shapes in perfect balance, hands sensitive to the tactile charm of objects, instincts that envelop every new form with introspective imagination. Yet it may be useful to remember that Cubism did not emerge out of nothing, that it is as much a legitimate and logical product of early twentieth-century thought and the human condition as Freudian depth-psychology or Einstein's theory of relativity.

To a senior member of the Paris Municipal Council, the Cubists in 1912 were just "a band of malefactors who behave in the world of art like the Apaches in ordinary life" and who should not have been allowed the use of the public building where, at the Salon d'Automne, they exhibited their hotly debated works. Retrospectively, we see them as a group of heroes who rescued art from a blind alley. When Lipchitz praised Cubism as "a new view of the universe," he did not exaggerate. It certainly offered a new view of art, or more precisely, it resuscitated a view of art that had been buried under heaps of artifacts.

Every history of art quotes Cézanne's letter admonishing his young admirer, the painter Emile Bernard, to "treat nature by means of the cylinder, the sphere, the cone." That the Cubists, led by Picasso, broke down the natural form of the object into its geometric elements is a minor fact. What is more significant is that they felt it a right, and even a duty, to rearrange these elements according to the patterns they wished to create. They felt free to transform a natural object into a figurative object that obeyed its own laws. The Cubists knew, and wanted the world to know, that a work of art is an organism, not a slavish imitation of something already in existence. While some of the Impressionists were still alive and very active, eager to reproduce nature with faithful adherence to perceptions of the eye, the new generation was less positivist, more skeptical, unwilling to trust direct sensation. It may also be noted that while Monets and Pissarros were at last fetching high prices, the "angry young men" of 1914 were being most critical of them — for example, the Austrian writer Hermann Bahr called Impressionism the falling away of man from the spirit, and charged it with being man lowered to the position of a gramophone record of the outer world. All that seemed to matter now was the "spiritual in art," to quote from the title of Kandinsky's belligerent pamphlet. And though the Cubists, except for Lipchitz, were agnostics or at least indifferent to religion, there is something deeply religious about their concern for the spirit which forms in contrast to the senses which deform. Strong-willed, almost ruthless rebels as the Cubists appeared, they revealed a profound sentimentalism as they concentrated on elegiac attitudes of single, compact figures, posed as though lost in a dream. It might be a man with a guitar, a Pierrot, or a Harlequin. "The tension set up between an intellectual mode of expression and a sentimental subject matter is one of the most violent and surprising in the history of art," was the observation of Andrew C. Ritchie.

"Introvert" is an odd term to apply to an aesthetic developed by a man as worldly as Picasso, yet it is correct to say that Cubism spelled the end of an art that had become very "extrovert," and that the Cubists, like certain medieval philosophers, were intent upon the essence rather than the appearance of things. One is reminded of the German mystic, Meister Eckhardt:

"If you seek the kernel, then you must break the shell, and if you would know the reality of Nature, you must destroy the appearance, and the farther you go beyond the appearance, the nearer you will be to the essence."

Lipchitz came to Cubism after having discovered for himself the ecstatic visionary, El Greco. There were other catalysts—a great deal of prehistoric, archaic, and medieval art, and African Negro sculptures. Lipchitz' most African work is a large standing figure of 1930, a garden sculpture over seven feet high, reminiscent of a totem. It has an unforgettable hypnotic stare. He had looked with fascination at the newly rediscovered *Sketchbook* of the architect Villard de Honnecourt, who was active between 1225 and 1250. An excellent draftsman, filled with intellectual curiosity, de Honnecourt had drawn animals and humans geometrically, constructing them from forms such as circles, triangles, and even pentagrams. Whatever art Lipchitz liked (which included Géricault, nineteenth-century Romantic painting, and the Pointillists) had to be poetic art, not in the sense of having the literary content of a fable, but in being an image created by a fertile mind, a configuration different and distinct from photographic verisimilitude.

He came to Cubism long after its first, analytic, phase was over. By 1914 Picasso and his colleagues had gone beyond reducing objects to their abstract components, beyond scrutinizing the external world. Four years had passed since Picasso with his bronze *Woman's Head* had shattered the volume of a skull into irregular facets and had reconstructed the shape in a free, unhampered rhythm. Lipchitz' *Sailor with Guitar* (1914) was preceded by such Cubist sculpture as La Fresnaye's *Italian Woman* (1912), Archipenko's *Walking Woman* (1912), Duchamp-Villon's *Lovers* (1913), and Boccioni's *Unique Forms of Continuity in Space* (1913).

La Fresnaye, Duchamp-Villon, and Boccioni died young, and Archipenko went his own way after a brief association with the movement. Many years after the inception of Cubism, none of the sculptors, not even Henri Laurens, could legitimately have said, "I am still a Cubist. . . . " To choose the Cubist sculptor *par excellence* from that score of young men who followed in the wake of Picasso's aesthetic credo, one must point to Lipchitz. His is the later, more mature, synthetic Cubism which summarizes an object rather than splits it into fragments. By 1913, when Lipchitz had cautiously started to use such Cubist devices as representing convex forms by concave ones, the rebels around Picasso and Braque had long abandoned decomposition in the plastic image for the gradual reappearance of the object, though nothing was further from their aims than a return to the portrayal of "reality" as practiced by the academicians.

In 1966 Lipchitz' Cubist sailors, bathers, musicians, or the vertical, blocklike orchestrations of stone he fashioned between his twenty-third and thirty-fifth years are no longer startling to us who have become accustomed to the innovations of a younger generation of sculptors—Armitage, Butler, Hare, Lippold, Mirko, and others whose abstract or near-abstract creations are hard to read. Lipchitz' Cubist work, on the other hand, has now become "classical" to such a degree that it is in demand even among collectors with conservative tastes. (It is, indeed, amusing to note how, with the passing of time, his Cubist figures have come to be accepted, even admired, while the focus of controversy has shifted to more recent works, and how today quite a few people extol his early Cubist creation at the expense of his later "baroque" work.) But in the context of his period, the young Lipchitz' progress was remarkable, from the meticulous finish of his first works, from naturalistically immaculate portrait heads and a gracious work like the 1912 *Woman with Gazelles*, to a work as unconventional, for the year 1914, as the *Sailor with Guitar*.

Superficially, a sculptor could profit very little from some of the Cubist precepts. Lipchitz knew that Cubism was basically a painters' revolution concerned with the means of transferring depth and volume onto a canvas, and that sculpture had little to gain from it, having in its very nature all means at hand of achieving depth and volume. For instance, it was revolutionary for a painter to combine several views of an object in a single image, whereas a three-dimensional object can always be viewed in the round. But instinct and intelligence told Lipchitz that Cubism might very well turn out to be a proper instrument of freedom as well as discipline for him. Unsympathetic writers have maintained that Lipchitz' early Cubist works look like canvases by Picasso or Braque seen through stereoscopic spectacles. Be that as it may, Cubism taught the "Benjamin" (as Lipchitz called himself) of the group more essential things—first, how to shed concern with detail and to arrange and combine forms freely in order to achieve a maximum of allusive meaning and imaginative association. Second, it taught him how to make sculpture "as pure as crystal" (a wish expressed by Lipchitz in a conversation with the novelist Jules Romains).

There is a dancing lightness about these early creations, some tinged with a bit of humor, others with a faint melancholy. Slowly, more and more descriptive details (like the sailor's cap and blouse), more and more of the flowing curves are sacrificed to achieve an angular austerity reminiscent of the fugues of Bach. So many characteristics are omitted for the sake of perfect harmony and elegance that even the sex of a figure is no longer recognizable. Finally we get sharp-edged vertical abstractions that might have grown like stalagmites rising from the floor of a limestone cavern were it not for some subtle, almost unnoticeable, suggestion of a human feature.

At this point Lipchitz the humanist clearly felt that he had reached an impasse. He had taken away too much, had reached the bottom, and fearing that he might end up with nothing, he reversed his course. Without denying to the abstractionist members of his confraternity the right to produce shapes completely unrelated to the kingdom of man, he himself felt the need to make the widest use of all the possibilities afforded by the human form, by history, religion, legend, allegory. If he were given to taking issue with what his friends write about him, he would heartily disagree with the poet Juan Larrea—"Many of your works are beautiful by virtue of being incomprehensible." Lipchitz would not allow anyone to consider a work of his beautiful because of the absence of comprehensibility, though the subject matter of some of his sculptures is not instantaneously recognizable. He wants to reproduce Man for man's sake, with the help of the humanistic intellect. As he once told Maurice Raynal:

"I admire an egg as a perfect product of nature ideally shaped for its purpose and its means for entering the world. But I am not a hen. I do not want to lay an egg."

Half a century ago Cubism was deplored in some quarters as anti-humanistic, as a mechanistic school threatening to drive the soul out of art by reducing natural forms to a schematic orchestration of voids and solids, straight lines and curves, concavities and convexities. Today we see it differently. Cubism began in a world dominated by the machine—the first decade of Cubism was over-shadowed by gigantic preparations for modern warfare, and thereafter by an internecine struggle fought more by tanks, airplanes, and submarine than by individual men. Bourdelle's and Maillol's reactivations of Greek art did not provide the symbols required in such a gruesome and complicated world. The Cubists came much closer to modern ballistics, functional architecture, and post-Euclidian mathematics—the achievements of a vigorously aggressive age in which the engineer and the boxer were more popular than the artist or the poet. The Cubists seemed on the surface to collaborate with the forces in power. Yet, looking over the painting or sculpture of Lipchitz and his fellow Cubists, one cannot avoid thinking of them as a humanistic "fifth column" carrying the conviction of the soul's superiority and inviolability. "The Cubists," said Andrew C. Ritchie, were very anxious to "place a heart in the machine, to discover Pierrot in the Robot."

There is a heart beating inside the objects Lipchitz shaped of stone or metal; these objects charm us with their lyrical flourish, or, like African idols, mesmerize us with a ritualistic fixity. They are as acceptable to us as Donatello, classic work upon which we can look in calm silence.

Lipchitz' Cubist sculpture, however, is not silent. It proclaims in glyptic terms the old and yet always new wisdom—a work of art is a metamorphosis of reality. In its highest stages, it represents a reality of its own, juxtaposed to nature. Once Lipchitz had learned this wisdom with all its ambiguous and often paradoxical ramifications, he graduated successfully from the school that Cubism had been for him. Pointing to a bronze transparency of 1926, *Pierrot Escapes,* he said of the clown about to climb a rope ladder from a prison window, "This is myself escaping from the imprisonment of Cubism."

He must have smiled as he said this. For Cubism underlies all his work. It can be felt in the tension of the struggle between geometry and human anatomy, in all his efforts to wed philosophical meaning to significant form. Looking back on his achievements at the end of his first creative phase, he summed them up in this way:

"I created what is the aim of all modern sculpture, that is, an object which is autonomous in nature and parallel with it."

As a septuagenarian he has not renounced the validity of his juvenilia for he recognizes their merits, their Dionysian energy balanced by an Apollonian calm of reason. The humanity, too, is the same. The man who dances, plays the guitar, or treads the stage to entertain war-weary crowds is brother to that Prometheus who is committed to human values in defiance of inimical forces.

Lipchitz' bodies appear as if they
had just been created out of earth by God's hands,
carrying with them still all the qualities of earth
in their heavy, massive shapes.

W. R. VALENTINER

The public, and often enough the critics as well, would have a painter or sculptor stand still after reaching maturity, repeating over and over the style of work it has become accustomed to expect, work that no longer offers much difficulty to the understanding. But when does an artist stop growing? Perhaps only on his deathbed. To a degree, every artist might say of himself, as Picasso did, "I do not seek, I find." In a recent statement Lipchitz explained to those who might be puzzled by the never-ending variety in his work that its elements were two—a solid foundation, and a lyrical expansion—and that his art expanded as every encounter enriched it:

". . . the encounters of materials, the encounters of ideas, the encounters between myself and things not-myself, and the encounters of various sides of myself. Sometimes these encounters are between similarities and likes; sometimes between opposites or wildly different things. But encounters are unpredictable, and through them the fabulous may take shape. From the encounter in the mind comes something that is unpredictable until then."

Just at the time when Lipchitz' Cubist work began to find more acceptance, and the original fierce opposition simmered down, new encounters changed his style almost overnight, disconcerting his then already numerous admirers. The series of "transparencies" was initiated by the *Seated Man* of 1925, which has an open space in its center. Although a decade earlier Lipchitz had carved a hole through the middle of the *Man with a Guitar*, it had been an isolated attempt to produce a focus of contrast. To the post-Cubist Lipchitz, the piercing of the mass became more and more important. He used ribbons of metal to enclose a void, and produced arabesques by freely alternating solids and voids. Many years later, Henry Moore, who is younger and cannot have remained uninfluenced by the "transparencies," became fascinated by the "mystery of the hole" and wrote that an opening could have as much shape and meaning as a solid mass.

To free himself from the inhibiting and repressive laws of gravity, to conquer the static force of weight by light and flight, has been the dream and hope of every creative man. But, as Leonardo confided to his notebooks, the sculptors can "neither represent transparent bodies nor luminous bodies nor angles of reflection nor shining bodies such as mirrors and like things of glittering surface, nor mists nor dull weather, nor an infinite number of things which I forbear to mention lest they should prove wearisome."

Modern sculptors, however, have exploded this ponderous denigration of their art. "I soar with this heavier-than-air," Lipchitz wrote to the critic Roger Vitrac at the climax of his "transparent" period. The transparencies came after the Cubist period, and they have, indeed, something in common with Futurism. While Lipchitz could not but resent the militaristic, radically anti-traditional, and in some ways proto-Fascist philosophy of some members of the Futurist group, he must have felt a kinship with their dynamism, with their vehement insistence on movement, on speed. Lipchitz, who works fast, loves clay because with it he can work out technical and aesthetic problems quickly before "the angels have flown away."

A reincarnated Leonardo might not consider Lipchitz' works to be sculpture, but might still concede that twentieth-century man is able to represent "an infinite number of things," far beyond the scope of the Quattrocento man. In fact, Lipchitz has to such an extent expanded technically the realm he has staked out, that conservative souls to whom a sculpture is a not too free reproduction of a standing figure are puzzled time and again by Lipchitz' work. For the timorous, of course, the work of Alexander Calder and others who gained strength and confidence from Lipchitz' experimentation (and often went beyond him in boldness) is even more bewildering.

Yet, Ruskin's broad definition of sculpture could be applied here, namely, that sculpture consists of the "reduction of any shapeless mass of solid matter to an intended shape." A narrower definition would not encompass the most widely known of the transparencies, the *Joie de Vivre*, an abstract grouping suggesting a man and woman dancing in great happiness. It is a bronze garden sculpture, over seven feet high, commissioned by a French collector in 1927. The subject matter is remarkable in that it indicates a new trend. Gradually the solitary figures in Lipchitz' work give way to groups of two. These are lovers or combatants, couples in embrace, and many mother-and-child groups. *David and Goliath, Rape of Europa, Prometheus Strangling the Vulture,* the titles alone make clear that there is thesis and antithesis, or at least the adjustment of one organism to the demands of another. Plastically, this schematic change results in a greater dynamism, in structural complications that create new challenges and temptations but also obscure the readability of each new work. The biographers have done their share to explain by a variety of personal conflicts or political reasons the "dualistic philosophy" in the work Lipchitz produced in the decade before World War II. Yet to one who sees a Lipchitz retrospective show today, the works themselves are far more important than the maker's motivations. *David and Goliath* and *Jacob Wrestling with the Angel,* we are told, were provoked by the tragedies in Hitler Germany. *Prometheus Strangling the Vulture* was made for the Palace of Discovery and Inventions at the 1937 World's Fair in Paris, and its symbolism is very clear—Prometheus, choking the giant vulture with one hand and defending himself from the bird's claws with the other, wears the Phrygian cap, a symbol of democracy.

Yet the public, which so enormously enjoys reading about an artist's emotional conflicts, his struggles with authorities, or his endeavors just to keep alive and working, cannot draw help from such entertainment when confronted with an artistic work itself. Michelangelo's *David* or *Moses* does not recall the intrigues and technical obstacles the artist had to cope with, and its majesty is neither enhanced nor impaired by any of the anecdotes that have been circulated in the past four centuries. If in *David and Goliath* the monster bears a swastika on his neck, this detail may very well enable posterity to date the sculpture, but it is doubtful that much is gained aesthetically by such a journalistic concession to readability.

The fact remains that Lipchitz was far more anguished in the thirties than during his Cubist period. Asked in 1930 whether he could return to the creations of his youth, he replied: "Even if I *wanted* to make something different, I could not. At this time I *cannot* make anything but monsters." (Marsden Hartley spoke of the "apocalyptic quality" of Lipchitz' work.)

Plagued by "monsters," as was Goya long before him, Lipchitz from about 1930 onward, producing much sculpture that might be termed programmatic. The danger in this lies in giving attention to subject matter to the detriment of form. On the whole Lipchitz has come out well, for he is always preoccupied with the problem that has concerned his colleagues in all ages, the relation of mass to space. He has tried to solve it differently in each stage of his career, but he has always known how far to go in the direction of realism and its opposite—how to turn his messages into mystic metaphors sufficiently abstract to bring us to a wondering halt, yet sufficiently evident to make us understand the meaning. He might have erred more frequently by letting the subject matter outweigh aesthetic considerations had he not, as a Cubist apprentice and master, achieved the freedom vis-á-vis nature that enabled him to turn his art into a newly shaped instrument for interpreting social and political development.

But it may also be wise at this point to stress the link with Rodin, and through him, with more than two thousand years of European sculpture, back to Phidias. As a young man Lipchitz could not have admitted, as he did years later, that Rodin was one of the two geniuses "to whom we owe our completely renewed vision" (the other was Cézanne). When Lipchitz arrived in Paris, the rebels were angry with Rodin, for they saw that he was old, vain, tired, and that he had for a long time stopped taking even the smallest part in carving his marbles and was leaving to his assistants the translation of his clay models into stone. At that time, the rising generation of artists despised Rodin as a peasant who lacked the intellect to discipline his creations into aesthetically impeccable forms, who looked for melodramatic effect, rhetorical antithesis, and whose only contribution was the ability to express pathos through the body.

In his middle years, Lipchitz, producer of baroque protuberances with a surging movement of dramatic force, knew not only Rodin's flaw (his frequent lack of interest in composition as a whole) but also his merit. Lipchitz does not have the Impressionist sculptor's passion for light and shade and, knowing that what an artist does is more important than what he says, he does not dwell on Rodin's regretable statement that the only principle in art is to copy what one sees. Lipchitz understands that Rodin's valid work resulted from the same freedom to exaggerate and distort that he himself considers an integral part of the modern sculptor's Bill of Rights. There is Expressionism in both the post-Impressionist Rodin and the post-Cubist Lipchitz, revealing an amazing kinship between their animated, tension-fraught bronzes.

The one big difference is that Rodin had exhausted his *élan vital* long before he reached sixty and little of great significance came from him during his last twenty years, whereas Lipchitz knows no letdown in vitality and intensity. There is another difference—the lessons Lipchitz learned as a Cubist have left their mark of discipline upon nearly everything he has done since 1926, however remote it might be from the orthodox Cubist severity and "pure form." In Rodin, however, moments of constructive insight alternate with moments in which fascination with a sensuous appeal or intellectual tickle overthrew the necessary balance. In a wise moment Rodin might realize that his sculpture was good because it was geometrical, and he would emphasize the interaction of plane and volume, but in the next moment he could surrender all geometry to any instinctual urge.

Without being the greater artist, Lipchitz has the better intellect of the two. However violent the gestation may be, it never completely destroys the will-to-form. An American critic, E. M. Benson, at the time of Lipchitz' first one-man show in the United States (in 1935) wrote:

"Each new piece of sculpture represented new problems which he solved, without equivocation, freshly and ingeniously. . . . Lipchitz found . . . that the physical laws which determined human anatomy also controlled plant and animal morphology and that it was the sculptor's job to translate these universal laws into organic, sculptural terms. . . . "

In this respect Lipchitz was as "old-fashioned" as any of the teachers at the Ecole des Beaux-Arts and as strict as the most conservative of his colleagues. But there were those in France who could not see the structure beneath the surface and who did not like the philosophy of freedom and humanity, expressed in an unusual language through sinuous forms.

Along with the *Prometheus* which they removed in a frenzy of xenophobia and ignorance, they might have removed much of the sculpture in the Musée Rodin. For, in the violent explosions that burst through his surfaces, Rodin was as "un-Latin" as Lipchitz and as "indecent." In the work of both men, two figures often coalesce in the ardor of their embrace (Lipchitz' *The Couple*, of 1929, had to be withdrawn from an open-air sculpture exhibition in Holland after the local burgomaster had been bombarded with protests). In the work of both men, figures are often locked together in an act of violence, and dark, ritualistic forces seem to be at work.

Lipchitz was bound to outdo even the titan Rodin in force of movement and kinetic quality. *The Return of the Prodigal Son*, produced in 1931, is still rather restrained; there is little movement as the curving shape of father and son become an indivisible unity. Yet some eight years later, in *Rape of Europa*, a continuous zigzag movement undulates swiftly through the bulbous forms, strongly emphasizing the violence of action attained by means of the ever-shifting light caught in the round bosses and hollows. This is one of Lipchitz' finest baroque studies. It was made on the eve of a war that was to engulf first nearly all of Europe and thereafter almost every region in the civilized world.

You will make alive all that you touch.

MAX JACOB
to JACQUES LIPCHITZ

In 1940 Lipchitz fled from the German armies advancing on Paris to the unoccupied south of France. But he had every reason not to feel safe there, and in 1941, having lost most of his possessions, he emigrated to America, taking along a couple of recently finished plaster casts, a portfolio of drawings, and, of course, a name that was respected by connoisseurs in the art capitals of the world. He had become a French citizen and considered himself a Parisian; like Chagall, Léger, and other French artists, he did not believe that he would stay permanently in the United States but planned to return to Europe after the war ended. He did go back to France in 1946, but a variety of reasons persuaded him that his home was now in New York, that he must return to the country that had given him refuge, and that he would strike firm roots in America's cultural soil.

At seventy-five, Lipchitz, looking back over twenty-five years spent in the United States, has every reason to be satisfied with his achievements. While the first years in the New World were lean ones financially, he gained many admirers through the one-man shows given him at Curt Valentin's Buchholz Gallery. Several commissions for works on a major scale were the result of his growing fame. Among the outstanding sculptures done in this American period are a new version of *Prometheus Strangling the Vulture* for Rio de Janeiro; a baptismal font for the church at Assy, Haute-Savoie (France); *The Birth of the Muses* for Mrs. John D. Rockefeller, III; and *Spirit of Enterprise*, for Philadelphia's Fairmont Park. Other bronzes inspired by political events of these two decades are *Prayer* (a grim reminder of the slaughter of Jews in Europe) and *Miracle* (a joyous response to the creation of a Jewish state).

These pieces indicate a profound change. It would not be correct to say that during his purely Cubist phase Lipchitz had worked with no concern for moral or social considerations, for there is a silent demonstration even in his early "heroes," who were humble folk, such as sailors, harlequins, and clowns (Picasso, creator of *Guernica,* as a young man also liked to choose his subjects from among the lower strata of society). But between 1926 and 1940 there is an increasing preoccupation with socio-philosophical themes, although certain examples might still be relegated to the "Art for Art's Sake" category. The American Lipchitz, in any event, never sees "Art" and "Life" as a dichotomy. For him the substance of art is life itself, and he is not enthusiastic about those who want the artist to withdraw into that pure form which is separated by a wide, unbridgeable gulf from the precarious existence of other beings.

Lipchitz has always been a humanist. As a young man he was repelled by the austerity of Brancusi's almost complete abstractions. Deliberately Lipchitz moved away from a point as close to abstraction as any artist, excepting Brancusi, had ever reached. Now he insists that he always conceives and executes his works "with the people in mind," that art is "made of blood—earth—all that is most concrete." He once aptly defined his goal:

"My desire is to make objects which embody all that is distinctive of man and at the same time so natural that nature will not blush before them."

Since avant-garde critics in recent years have occasionally deplored the baroque opulence and effervescence of Lipchitz' late style, a word on the meaning and significance of art might be in order. The critic who applied the word "hysteria" to this phase of Lipchitz probably prefers the cool detachment of those who emphasize only the sensuous qualities in a work of art, the pleasure-giving forms, and reject all meaning as "literature." The truth, however, is that all works of art have form. If they express human, cultural values, they are bound to be superior to those that merely satisfy the senses. Art, on higher levels, expresses and sometimes creates values, qualities upon which our way of life depends. Lipchitz' emotionalism, *per se,* need not be questioned. All that can concern the critics is whether what is expressed is offered in an aesthetically impeccable form; whether the artist, trying to probe into the meaning of human existence, has been able to transmute social values into significant form.

To present this "new" baroque Lipchitz, I have chosen to discuss in greater detail his *Prometheus,* because in Lipchitz' work it occupies approximately the place of *Guernica* in the *oeuvre* of Picasso. From Lipchitz' own statements we know that the legend of Prometheus had intrigued him long before 1933, the year he made the first sketches. His first *Prometheus* was a triumphant figure, guardian of the flame. The second, for the Paris World's Fair of 1937-38, was a warrior, still in the thick of battle and unsure of triumph. Lipchitz was very much disturbed at that time not only by the demonic forces that had taken over Germany, but also by the infiltration of an anti-humanist poison into his own beloved France. Yet always his problems were twofold—how to respond as a man to the violent conflicts in the modern world, and at the same time, how to give proper shape to the monsters haunting him.

"In the first sketch (1936)," he wrote, retrospectively, "Prometheus choked the vulture with his hands. From the standpoint of composition, this created a volume which warped the ensemble. I then tried to overcome this by having him choke the vulture with one hand only, and use the other to defend himself against the claws of the bird. In this way the composition became more eloquent at the same time that it opened up space and permitted one to see the depth."

Lipchitz created his own version of the myth. Prometheus' battle with the vulture is nowhere described in ancient literature. Zeus punished the rebel by chaining him to Mount Caucasus, where a vulture fed on his liver. Eventually, Heracles, with the consent of Zeus, killed the bird and set Prometheus free.

The World's Fair *Prometheus* was destroyed in 1938, after French city officials had it removed from its last site, on the Champs-Elysées. It was re-created in 1943-44, after the artist had found refuge in the United States—thus revealing itself as a symbol of one man's determination to carry on his task. The Brazilian government commissioned it for the facade of the new Ministry of Health and Education in Rio de Janeiro. But there was a new frustration. Due to misunderstanding, instead of the twenty-foot enlargement the artist had planned, a seven-foot model was cast, and it was too small for the very large facade. A third large plaster model was finished some time later, and from this model a bronze was made, eight-and-a-half feet high, for the Philadelphia Museum of Art.

With its absolute minimum of facial and bodily expression, its abstract cloud shapes, the *Prometheus* is unmistakably of our time. A Bernini would have produced something more explicit, and yet his name comes to mind. Both artists have a theatrical conception, both dematerialize the plastic volume by dissolving the mass in fluid atmosphere, both give animation to their work by exploiting the play of light and shadow (which in the *Prometheus*, intensifies the notion of struggle). Both have that dynamic vitality that is alien to the static principle of classic sculpture. Both have prepared the ground for the kinetic sculpture that has led to the mobiles of Calder.

The *Prometheus* is representative of a large number of works in which mythological themes are creatively transformed by Lipchitz to serve as symbols for events that hold fright and distress for the men and women of our century. But while making successful use of these metaphors, while treating modern subjects under the guise of ancient fables, the artist also immersed himself in a universal theme—maternity. A small Cubist bronze of 1914-15 is related to highly stylized Gothic statuary. In some ways the trio—the mother with one child on her lap and another on her shoulders—is also reminiscent in its totem-like structure and vertical formation of ancestor sculpture from Oceania.

While there is something cheerful and uplifting in this slender, still very representational work, the 1929-30 version of Mother and Child is characterized by anguish. A huge bird seems to be carrying on its back another animal-like creature, a child with huge, heavy arms. The mother's face (as in some African masks) has no mouth. She has no hands, only stumps of arms. When first shown, she appeared monstrous to many people, and spectators were as offended by this group as, about the same time, they were by Epstein's *Genesis*. In London, people who would have preferred the millionth variation of a chorus-girl Venus were repelled by Epstein's rendering of a heavily pregnant woman with a face like a chimpanzee. In France, they would have preferred neo-classic treatments *à la* Maillol or Despiau. Yet people with more intuition and introspection quickly realized that Lipchitz wanted to show humans as kin to animals in their helplessness, in their need for simple, basic requirements—warmth, food, protection.

The Mother of 1929-30 is without hands. The one of 1941-45 is without legs. The asymmetrically placed child on her back clings closely to the woman's neck. With stumps of arms upraised in a futile gesture, she might be a symbol for those countless mothers who perished in Nazi concentration camps, along with the children they futilely tried to protect.

"Grotesque" is the word that comes to mind as one looks at these two sculptures. They are grotesque in using distortion, exaggeration, omission for purely artistic reasons. But are they ugly? Terms like "beautiful" and "ugly" have become meaningless in the non-Renaissance milieu in which the artist and ourselves have grown up. Berenson wished that Michelangelo had died after the completion of the Sistine Chapel ceiling ("How many distorted, heaving, bulging monstrosities we should have been spared!"). "Ugly" was the term thrown at Rodin when he scandalized France with the brutal *Man with the Broken Nose,* the head of an aging man whose battered features increased his tortured expression. "Ugly" was shouted at Rodin's *Old Courtesan,* whose decrepit bent body mourns the ruin of her beauty. Yet Rodin was no more dismayed than Lipchitz, who learned from this Rodin, as he did from others, that only that which was without character should be called ugly.

Beauty in the ordinary sense of the word disappeared from Lipchitz' work with the early *Woman with Gazelles.* It is idle to speculate whether it was the first World War and the disillusionment to follow that turned Lipchitz forever from the young worshiper of classic Greece into the philosopher in wax and clay who visualized *Homo sapiens* not as a demigod but as a thwarted, frustrated, wretched heap of bones and flesh into which the Creator had placed a tiny spark. This very spark makes all the difference, though, lifting his creatures, however agonized their faces and however mutilated their bodies, high above the idiots without spark presented by Dubuffet and other followers of *art brut.*

For while there is dread and predicament, there are also counterforces at work. There is the male principle, Prometheus, who challenges fate, and there is the female, Hope through self-sacrifice, there is the recumbent Hagar, shielding the child in her lap from the merciless sun of the desert. There is the Virgin which Lipchitz fashioned in the early fifties for the baptismal font of the little church of Notre-Dame-de-Toute-Grace at Assy, a mountain village in the French Alps. Conceived in a spirit of bliss, it was named by the sculptor *Notre Dame de Liesse,* Our Lady of Joy.

Peace and happiness emanate from the Mother-and-Child group of 1949, in which a descending rhythm creates a quiet unity of soft folds and gentle curves. It may well be that the tenderness in this work is the result of the wish-fulfillment that came to the artist late in life in the form of a satisfying marriage crowned with the birth of a child. Happiness and universal acclaim reached him when he was about sixty. But the decade to follow was not one in which he sat back idly to survey past achievements, nor was it for him to duplicate with slight variations and decreasing strength what he had created at the height of manhood.

Lipchitz is the *Homo faber,* incessantly trying out new media, new techniques. "After periods of tense and controlled work I feel a strong urge for a kind of free lyrical expansion that cannot be stopped." In the mid-twenties this took the form of the "transparencies." In 1952, after a fire had burned his studio in Manhattan and destroyed many works, including the first sketches for the Virgin of Assy, he conceived the *Variations on a Chisel.* He played wittily with a number of chisels, in which he had suddenly discovered aesthetic potentialities, combining several elements to produce small bronzes of a Centaur, a woman with a bird, a combat, or Hebrew ritual objects.

In 1957 he showed for the first time work to which he had given the name "semi-automatics." They were small bronzes that, in the motifs (such as Mother and Child, Man with Rooster, Dancer, Reclining Figure) did not depart much from earlier works. What was new was the way they were made—Lipchitz had molded them quickly, without visual control, as a blind man would, trusting the instincts of his clairvoyant fingertips. It was not a permanent method of working, but was only a way of liberating himself of a fruitful "obsession." And in 1959 his New York gallery presented another set of new small bronzes under the title *A la limité du possible,* a reference not to the human mind which is inexhaustible in its resources of ways and means, but to the lost-wax process which, as in these works, had given all it could in transforming the most delicate combinations of matter into bronze. In these experiments Lipchitz combined prefabricated objects and natural forms of all sorts, fusing together bits of wood, string, flowers, fabrics, bones in a manner more subtle, more poetic than any earlier fusions of ready-made objects. In the preface to his catalogue, Lipchitz warned:

"Sculptors will probably say it is not sculpture any more; poets, it is not poetry; and art historians, it is perhaps not art after all. I can say I made these bronzes with the passion and joy of discovery, and I am sure I have conquered for myself a little bit more freedom in the making of my art."

Lipchitz will go on with his quest for freedom, at one time giving birth to things which grow quickly between his fingers without any premeditation, and at another letting a thing grow in long years of search and thought. For he is the essentially creative man producing more and more of these "Suns which can be reached by hand," these "man-made companions with a human heart inside," always willing to submit himself to change, development, evolution, always aware of unrealized possibilities and approaching them freshly with discipline and hard work. A spiral progression can be noted in much of his mature work—there is some delay, even some waste. There is seeming return to past achievements, but there is, in actuality, a steady movement forward and upward. What his tomorrow will bring as a combination of pure conscious calculation with psychic "encounter" on a nonrational basis, no one knows. But it will be a Lipchitz, order and system, worth and value, shaped out of a world of disorder and chaos, a world often myopic to spiritual values.

Jacques Lipchitz then is the creative man par excellence, who constantly subjects himself to the process of change, and with disciplined work imposes symbolic order upon the chaotic world. Pegasus, the horse of the Muses, is one of his favorite symbols. As he shaped its rippling, chunky forms, it came to indicate concentrated energies high above the ordinary laws of nature, to stand for a winged creature trying to free itself from the laws of gravity. Lipchitz, working as he does with heavy, earthy material, has no other aim than to elevate himself and his fellow men into a sphere where gravitational mass becomes as airy as a song, a tune played on a lyre, or human thought, the noblest metamorphosis of mortal man.